# Bolivia

# WORLD BIBLIOGRAPHICAL SERIES
General Editors:
Robert L. Collison (Editor-in-chief)
John J. Horton                    Ian Wallace
Hans H. Wellisch        Ralph Lee Woodward, Jr.

**Robert L. Collison** (Editor-in-chief) is Professor emeritus, Library and Information Studies, University of California, Los Angeles, and was a President of the Society of Indexers. Following the war, he served as Reference Librarian for the City of Westminster and later became Librarian to the BBC. During his fifty years as a professional librarian in England and the USA, he has written more than twenty works on bibliography, librarianship, indexing and related subjects.

**John J. Horton** is Deputy Librarian of the University of Bradford and currently Chairman of its Academic Board of Studies in Social Sciences. He has maintained a longstanding interest in the discipline of area studies and its associated bibliographical problems, with special reference to European Studies. In particular he has published in the field of Icelandic and of Yugoslav studies, including the two relevant volumes in the World Bibliographical Series.

**Ian Wallace** is Professor of Modern Languages at Loughborough University of Technology. A graduate of Oxford in French and German, he also studied in Tübingen, Heidelberg and Lausanne before taking teaching posts at universities in the USA, Scotland and England. He specializes in East German affairs, especially literature and culture, on which he has published numerous articles and books. In 1979 he founded the journal *GDR Monitor*, which he continues to edit.

**Hans H. Wellisch** is Professor emeritus at the College of Library and Information Services, University of Maryland. He was President of the American Society of Indexers and was a member of the International Federation for Documentation. He is the author of numerous articles and several books on indexing and abstracting, and has published *The Conversion of Scripts* and *Indexing and Abstracting: an International Bibliography*. He also contributes frequently to *Journal of the American Society for Information Science, The Indexer* and other professional journals.

**Ralph Lee Woodward, Jr.** is Chairman of the Department of History at Tulane University, New Orleans, where he has been Professor of History since 1970. He is the author of *Central America, a Nation Divided*, 2nd ed. (1985), as well as several monographs and more than sixty scholarly articles on modern Latin America. He has also compiled volumes in the World Bibliographical Series on *Belize* (1980), *Nicaragua* (1983), and *El Salvador* (forthcoming). Dr. Woodward edited the Central American section of the *Research Guide to Central America and the Caribbean* (1985) and is currently editor of the Central American history section of the *Handbook of Latin American Studies*.

VOLUME 89

# Bolivia

Gertrude M. Yeager
*Compiler*

## CLIO PRESS
OXFORD, ENGLAND · SANTA BARBARA, CALIFORNIA
DENVER, COLORADO

British Library Cataloguing in Publication Data

Yeager, Gertrude M.
Bolivia.—(World bibliographical series; v.89).
1. Bolivia. Bibliographies
I. Title  II. Series
016.984


ISBN 1–85109–066–5



Clio Press Ltd.,
55 St. Thomas' Street,
Oxford OX1 1JG, England.

ABC-Clio Information Services,
Riviera Campus, 2040 Alameda Padre Serra,
Santa Barbara, CA. 93103, USA.


Designed by Bernard Crossland
Typeset by Columns Design and Production Services, Reading, England.
Printed and bound in Great Britain by
Billing and Sons Ltd., Worcester.

# THE WORLD BIBLIOGRAPHICAL SERIES

This series, which is principally designed for the English speaker, will eventually cover every country in the world, each in a separate volume comprising annotated entries on works dealing with its history, geography, economy and politics; and with its people, their culture, customs, religion and social organization. Attention will also be paid to current living conditions – housing, education, newspapers, clothing, etc. – that are all too often ignored in standard bibliographies; and to those particular aspects relevant to individual countries. Each volume seeks to achieve, by use of careful selectivity and critical assessment of the literature, an expression of the country and an appreciation of its nature and national aspirations, to guide the reader towards an understanding of its importance. The keynote of the series is to provide, in a uniform format, an interpretation of each country that will express its culture, its place in the world, and the qualities and background that make it unique.

## VOLUMES IN THE SERIES

# Contents

**Contents**

**Contents**

# Introduction

Bolivia is one of South America's two landlocked nations. It is a nation of striking geographical contrasts; from gaunt mountains and cold, arid highlands to undeveloped lowlands and dense tropical rain forests. The Andes mountain range is at its widest through Bolivia, and the western cordillera, with peaks of over 21,000 feet in height, forms an effective barrier between Bolivia and Chile. East of these mountains is the bleak Altiplano which is 12,000 feet above sea level. It covers ten per cent of Bolivia's area, but supports seventy-five per cent of the population. The mostly Aymará-speaking inhabitants of the Altiplano practice meagre agriculture. The principal crops are tubers; potatoes and oca in their dehydrated forms, *chuno* and *tanta,* are dietary staples. Peasants augment their farming by raising alpaca, llama and sheep. Most Altiplano residents are economically dependent on the mining industry, including tin, copper, silver and tungsten.

Bolivia's fertile valleys, the Yungas, are located on the eastern slopes of the Andes. The area is drained by the Beni River and the tropical climate supports cocoa, sugar, coffee and tropical fruit cultivation. The country is also dotted by other fertile valleys which support the oasis-like towns of Cochabamba, Sucre and Tarija. These areas enjoy semi-tropical and temperate climates and produce much of the food consumed on the Altiplano.

Well over seventy per cent of Bolivia consists of undeveloped tropical lowlands of the oriente, or east. Rainfall in the Santa Cruz region is high, but seasonal, and large sections of land suffer the alternating effects of drought and flood. By far the wealthiest section in terms of economic potential, this region supports only twenty per cent of the population. To stimulate growth the government actively encourages colonization. The result is a heterogeneous population of Asian, European, South African and Mennonite settlers as well as migrants from the western Altiplano region. Since the mid 1960s, Santa Cruz has enjoyed impressive growth and is quickly beçoming the economic heartland of Bolivia.

Bolivia is one of South America's poorest nations. It has a high infant mortality rate; 333 of 1,000 new-born babies die in the first year of life. Life expectancy is 45.7 years for adult males and 47.9 years for adult females. The population is seventy-five per cent Indian and divided between two main groups; the Aymará speakers and the Quechua speakers. About twenty per cent of the population is *mestizo* and five per cent is white.

Historically, Bolivia has suffered from three major problems. Its population has lived and continues to live in the wrong place for economic development, the Altiplano rather than the oriente. Secondly, Bolivia's great natural resources have been traditionally located in distant, inaccessible places. In the past, aggressive neighbours have occupied these regions and annexed them to their territory. Substantial progress has been made in integrating its native population into national life. Peasants, now landowners, practice agriculture for their own benefit rather than for absentee landlords. They have elaborated a system of marketing their agricultural surpluses and have adopted new technology in order to increase production. Significant peasant participation in the economy can be seen in the countryside: corrugated roofs, bicycles and radios are much in evidence.

A great pre-Inca civilization existed on the shores of Lake Titicaca in prehistoric times. In about 600 AD these Aymará-speaking people came into contact with Peruvian coastal influences which can be seen in the massive stone buildings and the beautiful textiles, pottery and metalwork associated with the Tiahuanaco culture. Around 900 AD a mysterious event took place and when the advancing Incas reached Lake Titicaca, they found the Aymará living among impressive ruins which they could not explain. The final conquest of the Aymará by the Incas occurred in the late 1400s. Although politically subject to the Incas the Aymará preserved their language and social structure. They accepted the Incas' state religion and fought for the empire, albeit under the command of Aymará officers. Less than fifty years later, in 1538, the Aymará came under Spanish control when the Inca state collapsed.

During the colonial period Bolivia (or Upper Peru as it was then known) was governed by the Spaniards from Lima. In 1776 Upper Peru became part of the new viceroyalty of the Río de la Plata which had its headquarters in Buenos Aires. The discovery of Cerro Rico, the silver mountain, in 1545, and the establishment of the great mining centre at Potosí, meant that there was a large Spanish presence in the Charcas area. To administer the mines Spain designated Chuquisaca (now Sucre) as its principal city in Upper Peru, because of its proximity to Potosí and supplies of agricultural produce and Indian labour.

The location of Potosí in the centre of Upper Peru and on a high plateau meant that all goods consumed were imported. From southern Peru to northern Argentina merchants, farmers and stockmen participated in the Potosí market. Highland settlements were established within Upper Peru in order to satisfy its needs. The Cochabamba valley expanded and became the main supplier of maize and wheat to the mines, while Aymará settlements extended into the Yungas to cultivate coca.

The colonial economy of Upper Peru, based exclusively on mining, was fragile and vulnerable to market pressures. The depression of the 17th century meant economic disaster for the region. Short-term upswings in mining, such as those of the 1780s, did not bring about general recovery. Wealth shifted away from mining and mine-related industries; La Paz, a city which grew not as a result of mining but of the expansion of its own agrarian hinterland, replaced Sucre as Upper Peru's major city and eventually became the *de facto* capital of the area. Bolivia would not recover from this depression until the end of the 19th century.

In the middle of this general depression and at a time of chronic political instability Bolivia gained its Independence, and so began what Charles Arnarde called its 'long and frightening history'. Until 1880 a series of military and civilian caudillos (leaders) ruled Bolivia. Caudillo politics followed a pattern whereby periods of dictatorship which provided some stability alternated with intervals of violent competition among several aspiring presidents. Bolivia, the nation, existed in name only; the country was reduced to a series of quasi-autonomous city states. Provincialism, the result of a rugged terrain and a lack of roads, served the ambitions of local élites. During this period, however, a number of government leaders did provide periods of peace and development.

The ten-year presidency of Andrés Santa Cruz (1830–40) allowed Bolivia to organize the political state, define its nationalism and commit itself to republicanism. Had Santa Cruz concentrated his energies on developing Bolivia, rather than pursuing union with Peru, strong foundations could have been established. 19th-century political observers believed the cause of Bolivia's chronic instability to be its general poverty. The absence of economic activity meant that it was most important to maintain control over the national treasury. Each caudillo easily found large numbers of clients who supported him in order to gain access to public office.

Bolivia also paid dearly for its internal disorder in the international arena. Relations with Peru remained strained up to 1880, the result of previous quarrels and mutual suspicions. In 1889 Bolivian–Chilean rivalries became open warfare. After Independence Bolivia was unable to develop its mineral-rich Pacific coastal provinces. Chilean entrepreneurs, with the support of the government, began to develop nitrate deposits in these areas. At first the Bolivians agreed to foreign development, but eventually they realized that the contract agreement with the Chileans was to their disadvantage. A dispute arose and in 1879 the Chilean government occupied the *litoral* in an act of clear aggression, triggering the War of the Pacific. Bolivia was unable to defeat Chile and in 1884 the mineral-rich coastal areas were ceded to Chile; Bolivia became a truly landlocked nation. The treaty of 1884 not only signalled the end of the war but also marked the beginning of Bolivia's quest for a port, and made the return to the sea a pillar of Bolivian nationalism.

Many historians believe that this humiliating defeat in the War of the Pacific ushered in a period of responsible political management. Economic recovery, however, also played a role in ending political anarchy. In the mid-1860s a small group of entrepreneurs invested in the mining sector. By the 1880s these investments had matured and mining had once again become the key industry. These civilian élites wanted a political atmosphere that would benefit economic development. From 1880 to 1930 Bolivia developed a number of political parties and a parliamentary form of government. Political stability attracted foreign attention and investment and Bolivia started to become an integral part of international capitalism. As Bolivian miners expanded their markets significant economic growth was experienced. During the Second World War increased tin sales brought unprecedented prosperity. Strong ties with the international markets also made Bolivia both dependent and vulnerable. When depression hit in 1929 the economy was severely damaged.

The civilian government of Bolivia was unable to maintain control over internal affairs in 1931 and 1932. As the situation worsened President Daniel Salamanca turned his attention away from economic matters and instead focused on a border dispute. What had been a minor dispute between Bolivia and Paraguay since colonial times had, by 1932, escalated into a major war.

The Chaco War (1932–35) was a watershed in Bolivian history. It destroyed the political system introduced in the 1880s and brought about the collapse of civilian government. New ideas, and the discussion of vital issues such as the Indian question, agrarian reform, nationalization of industries and economic dependency became the diet of the Chaco intellectuals, the 'Chaco Generation'. In the post-Chaco War years Bolivian politics were radicalized, and discussions which took place in this era prepared the way for a national revolution in 1952.

The Bolivian revolution was not the result of an uprising of the masses. In 1951 a political party, the National Revolutionary Movement (MNR) won the presidential election but was denied the right to take office. A few months later the MNR seized power through a *golpe de estado.* Once in power it rapidly introduced legislation that brought about a social revolution.

The MNR introduced four major reforms: nationalization of the tin mines, universal suffrage, agrarian reform and an education programme. To protect itself, the MNR purged and reduced the military and created independent militias. Victor Paz Estenssoro served as president, guiding MNR policy. He attempted to broaden MNR support by cultivating and politicizing the *campesino* class.

Between 1952 and 1964 the political atmosphere in Bolivia was highly charged and reforms and social reordering took place quickly. The hacienda, an institution which was the symbol of the racist repression of the Indian, was destroyed quickly as peasants seized land, turned out or assassinated landlords and stopped paying taxes. Indian communities replaced the haciendas and quickly these communities became syndicates allied with the Bolivian Confederation of Workers.

Paz Estenssoro realized the political potential of the peasantry. He also realized that the landholding peasantry would become a conservative force in Bolivia. As the MNR began to lose support among urban middle class sectors the importance of the peasantry to the MNR increased.

In 1964, shortly after being elected president for the third time, Paz Estenssoro was overthrown by the military. For the last twenty years Bolivia has had a series of military governments of both the right and the left. Yet the political, social and economic reforms introduced in 1952 have remained intact. Although Bolivia continues to suffer from a host of problems, the greatest problem, the integration of the masses into national life, has been achieved.

# The Country and Its People

1 **The Andean republics: Bolivia, Chile, Ecuador, Peru.**
William W. Johnson. New York: Time, 1965. 160p. maps. bibliog.
An illustrated introductory study of Bolivia and the greater Andean region. A four-page introduction accompanies photographs of life in modern Bolivia. This is an excellent pictorial volume which is also suitable for children.

2 **Area handbook for Bolivia.**
Thomas E. Weil, Jan K. Black (et al.). Washington, DC: US Government Printing Office, 1974. 414p. (Foreign Area Studies Handbook).
One of a series of guides prepared by the Foreign Area Studies Department of the American University, in Washington, DC, which presents a compilation of basic facts about social, economic, and political institutions and practices.

3 **Bolivia, a country profile.**
Cynthia Davis. Washington, DC: United States Agency for International Development (USAID), Office of US Foreign Disaster Assistance, Evaluation Technologies Inc., 1984. 42p. maps.
This work gives a brief sketch of Bolivia with an emphasis on recent natural disasters and various relief projects.

4 **Bolivia, the heart of a continent; a few facts about the country and its activities.**
William A. Reid. Washington, DC: Gibson Bros., 1916. 65p. maps.
A readable and enjoyable account of life in Bolivia in the early 20th century which contains numerous interesting comments about day-to-day life.

1

5 **Bolivia, a land divided.**
Harold Osborne. London, New York: Royal Institute of International Affairs, 1954. 144p. maps. bibliog. Reprinted, Westport, Connecticut: Greenwood Press, 1985. 154p. maps. bibliog.

A short introduction to Bolivia by a British diplomat. This was the first survey of modern Bolivia published in the English language and its aim was to present a concise, but complete, picture of political, social, economic and historical conditions for the non-specialist.

6 **Bolivia: land, people and institutions.**
Olen Leonard. Washington, DC: Scarecrow Press, 1952. 297p. bibliog.

This analysis of the culture and economy of Bolivia was written to bridge the gap between the traveller's account and the scholarly monograph. It relates Bolivia's history and geography to contemporary life.

7 **Bolivia: a profile.**
William E. Carter. New York: Praeger, 1971. 176p. bibliog.

An excellent, brief overview of Bolivian society by a famous Andean scholar. This work, although not intended for a scholarly audience, is essential reading for anyone interested in Bolivian culture.

8 **Bolivia: an undiscovered land.**
Jean Manzon, Miguel Angel Asturias, Fernando Diez de Medina, translated by Frances Hogarth-Gante. London: Harrap, 1961. 116p. bibliog.

A marvellously illustrated introduction to the folk culture of highland Bolivia. A text accompanies and explains the excellent photographs.

9 **The United States and South America, the northern republics.**
Arthur P. Whitaker. Cambridge, Massachusetts: Harvard University Press, 1948. 280p.

A discussion of Bolivia within the context of the Bolivarian republics, those South American nations liberated from Spain in the early 1800s by Simón Bolívar. It focuses almost exclusively on the mining of tin and the various historical partitions of Bolivia by its neighbours.

# Geography

## General

10 **Bolivia: land, location and politics since 1825.**
J. Valerie Fifer. Cambridge, England: Cambridge University
Press, 1972. 301p. maps. bibliog. (Latin American Studies, no. 13).
The best English-language work available about Bolivia. It combines a discussion
of historical development with geography, and stresses the relationship between
geography, economic development, territorial losses and history. This work
should be read by any scholar, diplomat or tourist who is interested in Bolivia.

11 **The central Andes.**
Clifford T. Smith. In: *Latin American perspectives: geographical
studies.* Edited by Harold Blakemore, C. T. Smith. London:
Methuen, 1971, p. 263-335. maps. bibliog.
A general introduction to the physical features of the central Andean region of
South America. It takes a pan-national view and stresses physical features rather
than national boundaries.

12 **Economic geography of South America.**
Ray H. Whitbeck, Frank E. Williams. Westport, Connecticut:
Greenwood Press, 1971. 3rd ed. 469p. bibliog.
Organized on the basis of countries and of geographical regions this volume
discusses physical features, the geographical regions, the people and the economic
resources of Bolivia. This is an update of the 1940 edition.

13 **Geography of Latin America.**
Fred A. Carlson. New York: Prentice-Hall, 1946. 556p. maps.
bibliog.
This basic text on the geography of South America adopts a country-by-country
approach. For Bolivia see chapter 13 (p. 218–42).

14 **Source book on South American geography.**
John M. Renner. Wellington, New Zealand: H. Smith, 1976.
200p. bibliog.
A book of lectures, essays and addresses dealing with topics in the field of
economic geography.

15 **South America: an economic and regional geography.**
Edward W. Shanahan. New York: Gordon Press, 1976. 320p.
maps. bibliog.
This is the latest illustrated edition of a standard text on the geography of South
America. It discusses the geographical features and the resources of South
America as well as its industries and the general economic life of its people.

16 **South America: international river basins, including a section on
rivers and lakes forming international boundaries.**
New York: United Nations, 1977. [not paginated]. bibliog.
Discusses international rivers and watersheds and considers Lake Titicaca and
various rivers in eastern Bolivia.

# Political

17 **Geopolítica en Bolivia.** (Geopolitics in Bolivia.)
Alipio Valencia Vega. La Paz: Librería y Editorial 'Juventud',
1965. 380p. bibliog.
Argues that the major goal of Bolivians is to bring about national unity and that
the only way Bolivia will achieve development is to conquer the difficult national
territory.

# Maps and atlases

18 **Bolivia.**
Ministerio de Transportes y Comunicaciones, Servicio Nacional de
Caminos, Departamento de Planificación. La Paz: El Servicio,
1982.
A road map of Bolivia.

19 **Bolivia: official standard names approved by the US Board on
Geographic Names.**
US Board on Geographic Names, Office of Geography, Department
of the Interior. Washington, DC: US Government Printing Office,
1955. 269p. (Gazetteer no. 4).
This is a gazetteer which contains 18,000 entries for places and features in Bolivia.
The entries include approved standard names and unapproved variant names. The
scale of map coverage is about 1:1,000,000, except for Potosí and La Paz, which
are covered on a larger scale. Information is arranged in print-out form and
organized by name, designation (whether it is a town, delta, waterfall, etc.),
latitude and longitude, administrative division and locational reference.

20 **Mapas** *campesinos* **en Bolivia.** (Bolivian rural maps.)
Nadia Carnero Albarrán. Lima: Universidad Nacional Mayor de
San Marcos, Dirreción de Proyección Social, Seminario de Historia
Rural Andina, 1980. 57 leaves.
A real property atlas of the Chaqui region.

# Tourism and Travel Guides

21  **Adventuring in the Andes: the Sierra Club travel guide to Ecuador, Peru, Bolivia, the Amazon Basin, and the Galapagos.**
Charles Frazier, Donald Secreast.   San Francisco: Sierra Club Books, 1985. 262p. maps. bibliog.

A guide to backpacking, trekking and camping in South America. It includes useful information on medicines, equipment, and suppliers, as well as information on day-trips and longer camping trips.

22  **Birnbaum's South America 1988.**
Stephen Birnbaum.   Boston, Massachusetts: Houghton Mifflin, 1987. 784p.

A useful tourist guide of South America which emphasizes comfortable travel.

23  **An occult guide to South America.**
John Wilcock.   New York: Book Division of Laurel Tape and Film, 1976. 222p. bibliog.

This holiday guide explores native religions, syncretic practices and occultism.

24  **South America on a shoestring.**
Geoffrey Crowther.   South Yarra, Victoria, Australia: Lonely Planet, 1986. 346p. maps.

This volume is aimed at those who wish to see South America on a small budget and enjoy themselves immensely. Although four-star accommodation cannot be found here, this travel guide does guarantee contact with local culture. This is a valuable book which is almost in the same league as the *South American handbook* (q.v.).

25 **South America: river trips.**
George N. Bradt. Cambridge, Massachusetts: Bradt Enterprises, 1981. 186p. maps. bibliog.

A travel guide to boating and water trips in South America. Useful tourist information is also included.

26 **South American handbook.**
Edited by John Brooks. Bath, England: Trade & Travel Publications, 1988. 64th ed. 1340p.

This is the bible of the South American traveller; the most complete and thorough tourist guide to South America. The Bolivian section (p. 162-209), includes a short history of the country, and practical information about money, hotels, dining out and transport.

27 **South American survival.**
Maurice Taylor. London: Wilton House Gentry, 1977. 272p. maps. bibliog.

A useful guide for the student or budget traveller which includes practical advice and useful tips for inexpensive travelling.

28 **Visit Bolivia.**
Regis Dunningan. Washington, DC: Pan American Union, Travel Division, 1956. 32p. map.

A dated, but still useful, aid for the Andean tourist.

# Travellers' Accounts

**29  Across the Andes, a tale of wandering days among the mountains of Bolivia and the jungles of the upper Amazon.**
Charles Johnson Post.   New York: Outing Publishing, 1912. 362p. maps.
This turn-of-the-century travellers' account is both highly interesting and readable.

**30  Adventures in Bolivia.**
Cecil Herbert Prodgers.   London: John Lane, 1922. 232p.
The story of an English expedition to the remote, and previously isolated, Challana Indians. The expedition took place during the rubber boom, in 1903, when the author was employed by the Challana and Tongo Rubber Company. The volume even includes lists of items of equipment needed on such an expedition.

**31  Bolivia, the central highway of South America, a land of rich resources and varied interest.**
Marie R. Wright.   Philadelphia: G. Barrie, 1907. 450p. map.
Compiled after a long residence in Bolivia, which included a thousand-mile muleback tour, this is an excellent turn-of-the-century travel account. It presents a positive image of Bolivia and dismisses its chaotic politics as the result of 'plenty of vigour' on the part of the people, and as a constant struggle against despotism.

**32  Bolivia: gate of the sun.**
Margaret J. Anstee.   New York: P. S. Eriksson, 1971. 281p. maps. bibliog.
This highly personal account is an attempt to set the record straight concerning Bolivia's unattractive foreign image. It is not an apology, but rather an attempt to capture the spirit of Bolivia.

**33 The Bolivian Andes; a record of climbing and exploration in the Cordillera Real in the years 1898 and 1900.**
Sir W. Martin Conway. New York: Harper Bros., 1901. 402p.

A personal account of an early journey of exploration through the Andes mountain range.

**34 Coups and cocaine.**
Anthony Daniels. London: John Murray, 1986. 230p.

A readable account of a 1981 odyssey through South America, including Bolivia.

**35 Eastern Peru and Bolivia.**
William C. Agle. Seattle, Washington: Homer M. Hill, 1901. 45p.

In this brief travel account, the author, an American engineer, provides data concerning ecological conditions in a major mining area. Although useful to historians, it was primarily prepared as a guide for those whose purpose in going to South America was to make money. A good introduction to the American mentality, set in the days of gunboat diplomacy.

**36 Exploration Fawcett.**
P. H. Fawcett. London: Hutchinson, 1953. 312p. maps.

The British edition of Fawcett's explorations during the rubber boom of the early 20th century.

**37 Exploration of the valley of the Amazon made under the direction of the Navy Department.**
William L. Herndon. Washington, DC: R. Armstrong, 1853-54. 2 vols. maps.

A richly detailed and interesting account of an expedition which was sent into Bolivia's Amazon Basin to collect scientific data.

**38 Green hell, adventures in the mysterious jungles of eastern Bolivia.**
Julian Duguid. New York: Century, 1931. 839p. maps.

An interesting, colourful and detailed account of a journey into Bolivia's tropical eastern zones.

**39 High spots in the Andes; Peruvian letters of a mining engineer's wife.**
Josephine Hoeppner Woods. New York: G. P. Putnam's, 1935. 320p.

This marvellous description of life in an American mining camp, from a woman's point of view, is rich in detail about the everyday life of the people and local culture.

40  **Journey through a forgotten empire.**
Mark Howell.  London: G. Bless, 1964. 200p.
A description of a British film crew's trip through the Inca empire from Cuzco in
Peru, and on into Bolivia. This modern travel account provides much detailed
information on contemporary life. It is a readable, personal narrative.

41  **The life of Sir Clements R. Markham.**
Albert Markham.  London: John Murray, 1917. 384p. map.
A personal, not scholarly, biography of a famous geographer.

42  **Lost trails, lost cities.**
P. H. Fawcett.  New York: Funk & Wagnalls, 1953. 332p. maps.
An illustrated account of life and travel in Bolivia during the rubber boom at the
beginning of this century.

43  **Papers from the notes of an engineer.**
Frederick Gleason Corining.  New York: Scientific Publishing,
1889. 103p. map.
A tale of mountain climbing in Bolivia.

44  **The route to Bolivia via the River Amazon. A report to the
governments of Bolivia and Brazil.**
George W. Church.  London: Waterlow & Sons, 1877. 216p.
A very interesting travel account by one of the most controversial foreign figures
in 19th-century Bolivian history.

45  **A search for the apex of America, high mountain climbing in Peru
and Bolivia, including the conquest of Huascarán, with some
observations on the country and the people below.**
Annie Smith Peck.  New York: Dodd, Mead, 1911. 370p. map.
A travel and adventure book with interesting information about social customs
and daily life from a woman's point of view.

46  **Six years in Bolivia. The adventures of a mining engineer.**
Anselm Verner Lee Guise.  London: T. F. Unwin, 1922. 246p.
map.
Recounts the experiences of a young mining engineer, who was the assistant
manager of a tin mine in the Oruro area. The work contains numerous references
to flora and fauna as well as descriptions of native life and local customs.

47  **South America: observations and impressions.**
James Bryce.  London: Macmillan, 1912. 512p. map.
A travel diary of a four-month trip through South America, which included
Bolivia (p. 166-204).

10

48 **Thunder beats the drum.**
John Hewlett. New York: R. M. McBride, 1944. 340p. map.

This journal chronicles the unsuccessful trip to locate journalist and explorer, Thomas Fawcett, in the Bolivian heartland. The Fawcett expedition had been commissioned by the Royal Geographical Society, in London, to explore South America. The explorers were supposedly swallowed up in the 'world's greenhouse'.

49 **Travels in various parts of Peru, including a year's residence in Potosí.**
Edmond Temple. Philadelphia: E. L. Carey, A. Hart, 1833.
2 vols. Reprinted, New York: AMS Press, 1971.

The American edition of Temple's account of his visit in 1825 to the mining zones of Upper Peru (or Bolivia) on the request of the Potosí, La Paz and Peruvian Mining Association. This is one of the classic traveller's accounts of the Andean area.

# Flora and Fauna

50 **Aggression during single animal introductions and group formations in the Bolivian squirrel-monkey.**
L. E. Williams, C. R. Abee.   *American Journal of Primatology*, vol. 8 (1985), p. 371-72.

The social organization of *Saimiri boliviensis b* is thought to be sexually segregated during non-breeding seasons. To investigate the influence of the social order on patterns of aggression, controlled single animals were introduced into established groups and these newly-created groups were studied in a scientific manner.

51 **Bats of Bolivia: an annotated checklist.**
Sydney Anderson, Karl F. Koopman, Ken G. Creighton.   New York: American Museum of Natural History, 1982. 24p. map.

This work, by a noted scholar, lists species of bats found in Bolivia.

52 **Birds of South America.**
John Gould.   London: Eyre Metheuen, 1972. 321p. bibliog.

The plates of the birds of South America contained in this volume were selected from Gould's four monographs. Gould was a natural history artist and a great ornithologist who lived during the 19th century. This work is as much a work of art as a work of science.

53 **Ethnobotany of the Chacobo Indians, Beni, Bolivia.**
Brian M. Boom.   In: *Advances in economic botany*, vol. 4. New York: New York Botanical Garden, 1987.

This entire volume of 68 pages discusses the medicinal uses of plants by the Chacobo Indians.

54 **A guide to the birds of South America.**
Rodolphe Meyer de Schauensee.   Wynnewood, Pennsylvania:
Academy of Natural Sciences of Philadelphia, 1970. 470p. bibliog.

The bird fauna of South America is the richest in the world both in numbers and in variety of species. This is an illustrated and systematic guide which can be used by both the professional and amateur ornithologist.

55 **Notes on Bolivian mammals.**
Sydney Anderson, William David Webster.   *American Museum Novitates*, vol. 2766 (3 Aug. 1983), p. 1-3.

Describes the first reporting of twenty-three bat species from the department of Pando.

56 **Plant hunters in the Andes.**
Thomas Harper Goodspeed.   New York: Tronto, Farrar & Rinehart, 1941. 429p. maps.

Discusses the collecting of plants and the mapping of vegetation in Peru, Chile, Bolivia and Argentina over a twenty-five year period. A second edition, available from the University of California Press, was published in 1961.

57 **Rodents from the Deseadan Oligocene of Bolivia and the relationships of the Caviomorpha.**
Bryan Patterson, Albert Edward Wood.   *Bulletin of the Museum of Comparative Zoology*, vol. 149, no. 7 (1982), p. 371-543.

Discusses rodents common in Bolivia.

58 **The species of birds of South America with their distribution.**
Rodolphe Meyer de Schauensee.   Philadelphia: Academy of Natural Sciences of Philadelphia, 1966. 577p. bibliog.

A modern one-volume listing of the birds which can be found in South America. The purpose of this work is to fill a gap in ornithological literature and to provide a study which is available to both the professional and amateur ornithologist alike. It provides a particularly useful study of distributional problems, and the numerous taxonomic notes should be of value to students of anatomy and systematics. Also included is a country-by-country bibliography.

59 **Three adventures: Galapagos, Titicaca, the Blue Holes.**
Jacques-Yves Cousteau, Philippe Diole, translated by
J. F. Bernard.   New York: Doubleday, 1973. 304p.

Describes how, after a difficult trip up the Andes to Lake Titicaca, the highest large navigable lake in the world, the Cousteau expedition descended into the lake in mini-submarines to search for its secrets and to test their equipment's performance at high altitudes.

# Prehistory
# and Archaeology

### 60 Ancient arts of the Andes.
Wendell C. Bennett.    New York: Museum of Modern Art, 1954.
186p. bibliog.

An introductory survey to the art of the ancient cultures of the Andean regions, which includes references to both the Tiahuanaco and Inca cultures of Bolivia. The work is divided into two sections. Section A presents an historical and chronological account. Section B discusses weaving, ceramic techniques and also includes some illustrations.

### 61 An archaeological investigation of the Lupaca kingdom and its origins.
John Hyslop.    PhD dissertation, Columbia University, New York, 1976. 473p. bibliog.

The first detailed account of Aymará life prior to their conquest by the Inca empire.

### 62 Art and time in the evolution of Andean state expansionism.
Anita Gwynn Cook.    PhD dissertation, State University of New York at Binghamton, New York, 1986. 351p. bibliog.

The figural iconography shared by the Huari of Peru and the Tiwanaku of Bolivia occurred during a two hundred year period – 500 AD to 700 AD. Important differences in the shape and details of the figures make direct comparisons difficult. The identification of attributes that characterized the two principal icons that occurred in both polities (the Staff Deity and Profile Attendant) are defined. Evidence of historical continuity from 200 AD to 700 AD helped to trace attributes that defined classes of similar figures during the periods of Huari and Tiwanaku expansion.

14

63  **Built before the flood: the problem of the Tiahuanaco ruins.**
    H. S. Bellamy.  London: Faber & Faber, 1943. 144p.

An interesting but thoroughly dated study of the Tiahuanaco problem. Factually this work is out of date, but it is valuable as a source of information on the importance and impact of the theories put forward by A. Posnanksy.

64  **The calendar of Tiahuanaco.**
    H. S. Bellamy, P. Allan.  London: Faber & Faber. 1956. 440p.

The purpose of this book is to prove that the relief on the great Gateway at Tiahuanaco is a calendar that is unique and one of the oldest in the world, having had its origins in 'another' world.

65  **Copacauana-Copacabana.**
    Julio María Elías.  La Paz: Santuario de Copacabana, 1978. 197p.

A history of the famous ceremonial-religious site on the shore of Lake Titicaca from pre-Columbian times to the modern era.

66  **Descripción sumaria del templete semisubterráneo de Tiwanaku.**
    (A brief description of the semi-subterranean temple of
    Tiahuanaco.)
    Carlos Ponce Sangines.  La Paz: Industrial Grafia E. Burillo, 1964.
    89p.

Provides a brief description of the archaeological site at Tiahuanaco. The extensive maps, charts and photographs provide the reader with a visual tour of the site and the temple. Based on excavations completed in the early 1960s by the Centro de Investigaciones Arqueológicas en Tiwanaku which Ponce Sangines headed.

67  **The domestication and exploitation of the South American camelids:
    methods of analysis and their application to circum-lacustrine
    archaeological sites in Bolivia and Peru.**
    Jonathan Dwight Kent.  PhD dissertation, Washington University,
    St. Louis, Missouri, 1982. 645p. bibliog.

Focuses upon the development of techniques to analyse faunal assemblages from archaeological sites containing the remains of camelids, with emphasis on the domestication of animals and trade. These methods are then applied to two archaeological sites in Bolivia and Peru.

68  **Excavations at Tiahuanaco.**
    Wendell C. Bennett.  New York: American Museum of Natural
    History, 1934. 494p. bibliog.

This study, by a well-known scholar, continues to be an excellent starting place for Tiahuanaco archaeological studies.

69 **Excavations in Bolivia.**
Wendell C. Bennett. New York: American Museum of Natural
History, 1936. 507p. maps. bibliog.

This work discusses archaeological research conducted in Bolivia between 1933
and 1934 which was, unfortunately, hindered by the Chaco War (1932-35).
Excavation took place at sites near La Paz and Lake Titicaca.

70 **The Great Idol of Tiahuanaco: an interpretation in the light of the
Hoerbiger theory of satellites, of the glyphs carved on its surface.**
H. S. Bellamy, P. Allan. London: Faber & Faber, 1959. 192p.
bibliog.

Endeavours to describe and interpret the glyphs which cover the surface of the
Great Idol at Tiahuanaco.

71 **History of the Inca empire.**
Bernabé Cobo, translated by Roland Hamilton, foreword by John H.
Rowe. Austin, Texas: University of Texas Press, 1979. 279p.

Hamilton located the original Cobo manuscript (dated 1653) in a church archive
in Seville, Spain. Here, he presents Books 11 and 12, which deal directly with the
native population and the government apparatus of the Inca state.

72 **Marsh resource utilization and the ethnoarchaeology of the Uru-
Muratos of highland Bolivia.**
Darwin David Horn, Jr. PhD dissertation, Washington University,
St. Louis, Missouri, 1984. 411p. bibliog.

Discusses two aspects of man's use of marshes. The author evaluates four
characteristics of marsh vegetation: abundance (in terms of rates of primary
productivity); nutritional composition; seasonal availability; and ease of harvest.
In terms of these factors, marshes have the potential to support human
populations. The second aspect of marsh utilization focuses on the Uru-Muratos,
highland Bolivians who continue to exploit marshes in a traditional manner.
Modern exploitation is also examined.

73 **The peoples and cultures of ancient Peru.**
Luis G. Lumbreras. Washington, DC: Smithsonian Institution
Press, 1974. 248p. maps. bibliog.

A recent survey of Andean archaeology, a field undergoing dramatic revision,
which was written to serve as the basic text for a course in Andean archaeology at
the University of San Cristóbal de Huamanga at Ayacucho, Peru. Aimed at the
student or non-specialist, but useful also for anthropologists specializing in other
areas.

74 **Prehistoria de Bolivia.** (Prehistory of Bolivia.)
D. E. Ibarra Grasso. La Paz, Cochabamba: Editorial los Amigos
del Libro, 1965. 327p. map. bibliog.

A standard introductory survey to the prehistory and archaeology of Bolivia
which discusses: palaeolithic Bolivia; Tiahuanaco in its ancient, classical and
expansion periods; the Nazcoide and Yampara cultures; Potosí; and the arrival of
the Inca empire. A second edition appeared in 1973.

75 **Del Tawantinsuyu a la historia del Perú.** (From Tawantinsuyu to the
history of Peru.)
Franklin Pease. Lima: Instituto de Estudios Peruanos, 1978. 245p.
bibliog. (Historia andina, 5).

A study based on the *visitas* (visits) made by colonial bureaucrats to the Aymará
kingdoms near Lake Titicaca, during the early colonial era.

76 **El Tawantinsuyu y el control de las relaciones complementarias.**
(The Inca empire and the control of complementary relations.)
Augustín Llagostera Martínez. *International Congress of
Americanists*, vol. 42 (1976); *Acts*, vol. 4 (1976), p. 39-50. bibliog.

77 **Toward the development of the Tiahuanaco (Tiwanaku) State.**
Edited by David L. Browman. In: *Advances in Andean
archaeology*. The Hague: Mouton, 1978, p. 327-50. 580p.
bibliog.

The archaeological work being carried out at Tiahuanaco continues at a
'tortuously' slow pace. The examination of Tiahuanaco mythology and religion
has led to several conclusions. It appears that Tiahuanaco advanced essentially by
relying on peaceful means and along the established trade routes.

# History

## General

78 **Almanaque histórico de Bolivia: selección de notas históricas, 1538-1979.** (Almanac of Bolivian history: a selection of historical notes, 1538-1979.)
Winsor López Videla. La Paz: Ediciones Burgos, 1980. 477p. bibliog.
This new historical almanac includes useful chronological and military information.

79 **The Andean past: land, societies, and conflicts.**
Magnus Mörner. New York: Columbia University Press, 1985. 300p. bibliog.
Using John Murra's thesis of reciprocity, Mörner traces social development from the earliest times through the colonial and national periods. There are three noteworthy features of the work: the coverage of the prehistoric period; the development of a regional study of Andean space rather than artificial nation-state divisions; a readable, and sympathetic treatment of the subject.

80 **Bolivia: the evolution of a multi-ethnic society.**
Herbert S. Klein. New York: Oxford University Press, 1982. 317p. maps. bibliog.
The best available historical survey of Bolivia in the English language, covering the social, cultural, economic and political evolution of Bolivia from the pre-Columbian era to the present time. It places special emphasis on the changing role of the Indian peasant and the changing nature of the Bolivian economy.

81 **Ensayos sobre la realidad boliviana.** (Essays on Bolivian reality.)
Mariano Baptista Gumucio. La Paz: Comité Nacional del
Sesquicentenario de la República, 1975. 217p.
A collection of previously unpublished essays by a well-known historian and
intellectual.

82 **Historia contemporánea de Bolivia.** (The contemporary history of
Bolivia.)
Mariano Baptista Gumucio. La Paz: Gisbert y Cía, 1980. 400p.
bibliog.
This work traces the history of Bolivia from 1930 to 1978. Major themes included
are the Chaco War, the development of a national intelligentsia, the national
revolution of 1952, and modern militarism and populism.

83 **Historia de Bolivia.** (History of Bolivia.)
Alfredo Ayala Z. La Paz: Editorial Don Bosco, 1976. 424p.
bibliog.
This factual outline of the history of Bolivia is a good place to begin learning the
basics of Bolivian historical chronology.

84 **Historia de Bolivia.** (History of Bolivia.)
Augusto Guzmán. La Paz: Editorial los Amigos del Libro, 1981.
6th ed. 454p. bibliog.
A prize-winning survey of Bolivian history which discusses in a chronological
framework the following topics: pre-Columbian cultures, the colonial period,
Independence, the Republic, the age of dictators and miners, and the revolution
of 1952.

85 **Historia económica de Bolivia.** (Economic history of Bolivia.)
Luis Peñaloza Cordero. La Paz: Editorial los Amigos del Libro,
1953-54. 2 vols. bibliog.
A good survey of the economic history of Bolivia.

86 **Historiografía boliviana.** (Bolivian historiography.)
Valentín Abecia Baldivieso. La Paz: Editorial 'Letras,' 1965.
628p. bibliog. 2nd ed. 1973. 588p.
An encylopaedic study of history and historical writing which provides bio-
bibliographical data for every historian of Bolivia, both professional and amateur,
from the 16th century onwards.

87 **The historiography of colonial and modern Bolivia.**
Charles Arnade. *Hispanic American Historical Review*, 1962,
p. 333-84.
This article remains the best single survey of historical writing in Bolivia.

88 **Nueva historia de Bolivia.** (A new history of Bolivia.)
   Enrique Finot. La Paz: Gisbert y Cía, 1980. 368p. bibliog.
An excellent interpretation of Bolivian history from the pre-Inca civilization of
Tiahuanaco to the 1930s. The topics discussed include Tiahuanaco and the Inca
conquest, the Spanish conquest of 1538 and the colonial era, the establishment of
the Republic, in 1825, caudillo politics of the 19th century, the War of the Pacific
(1879-84), the rise of the conservative élites, and the Chaco War (1932-35).

89 **150 years of Bolivian Independence.**
   Fernando Ortiz Sanz. *Americas* (Organization of American
   States), vol. 27, no. 8 (1975), p. 2-4.
Chronicles the history of Bolivia from Independence to the present day.

90 **Páginas escogidas.** (Selected pages.)
   Mariano Baptista Gumucio. La Paz: Editorial los Amigos del
   Libro, 1975. 388p.
A collection of writings and speeches by an important 19th-century political
figure, Mariano Baptista Caserta. This work discusses a variety of key historical
issues.

91 **Research guide to Andean history: Bolivia, Chile, Ecuador, and
   Peru.**
   Edited by John J. TePaske. Durham, North Carolina: Duke
   University Press, 1981. 346p.
A series of essays, and guides to archives and public and private libraries,
prepared by noted scholars in which useful information is presented in a readable
manner.

92 **A short history of Bolivia; being an account of all that has taken
   place in Upper Peru from earliest times to the present.**
   Robert Barton. La Paz: Editorial los Amigos del Libro, 1968.
   343p. maps. bibliog.
This useful history of Bolivia presents material in a straightforward manner and
follows political events. The four major periods of Bolivian history: ancient or
pre-Columbian, colonial, Independence and the 19th century, and the contemporary age, are given equal attention.

# Colonial period

93 **An abolitionism born of frustration: the Conde de Lemos and the Potosí mita, 1667-1673.**
Jeffery A. Cole. *Hispanic American Historical Review*, vol. 63, no. 2 (1983), p. 307-33.
This article examines the attempts made by Viceroy Conde de Lemos to abolish the Potosí mita, or forced labour system. What is clear to the author is that the 'flexibility' attributed to the Hapsburg bureaucracy also existed in the American colonies. The transformation of the mita from a draft labour system to a cash subsidy demonstrated that fundamental decision-making took place in the colonies.

94 **Acerca del sistema tributario pretoledano en el Alto Perú.** (On the pre-Toledan tribute system in Upper Peru.)
Tristan Platt. *Avances*, vol. 1, no. 1 (1978), p. 33-47. bibliog.
Traces the complexity of this era of transition (1532-70). It was during this period that the bases of the colonial system were consolidated in their Andean form.

95 **An Aymará kingdom in 1576.**
John Murra. *Ethnohistory*, vol. 15, no. 2 (1968), p. 115-51.
Murra's discussion of the Lupaca kingdom is based on interviews conducted in 1576 by Garci Diez de San Miguel, a Crown inspector sent to the Aymará areas of Upper Peru by the Spanish colonial authorities.

96 **Aymará lords and their European agents at Potosí.**
John Murra. *Nova Americana*, vol. 1 (1978), p. 231-43. bibliog.
Examines the role of traditional tribal leaders in the colonial economy of Upper Peru.

97 **Caciques, class structure and the colonial state in Bolivia.**
Brooke Larson. *Nova Americana*, vol. 2 (1979), p. 197-235. bibliog.
This exploratory essay on continuity and change in Indian communities from 1549 to the 18th-century Bourbon reforms, examines social stratification, as well as caste and class relationships. It is based on archival research.

98 **Coerced consumption in colonial Bolivia and Guatemala.**
Brooke Larson, Robert Wasserstrom. *Radical History Review*, no. 27 (1983), p. 49-78.
Examines the 'compulsory market' in colonial Guatemala and Charcas. Not content with normal revenue-producing measures, many colonial governors organized illegal and coercive trading activities which forced Indians to buy alcohol, textiles and other goods. Based on both archival research and secondary sources.

99 **Colonial silver mining; Mexico and Peru.**
David Brading, Harry Cross. *Hispanic American Historical Review*, vol. 52, no. 2 (1972), p. 545-79.
A very useful comparative study of silver mining, technology, labour systems, and production in the two principal areas of Spain's empire.

100 **Discontent with the Spanish system of control in Upper Peru, 1730-1809.**
Leona Ruth Auld. PhD dissertation, University of California, Los Angeles, 1963. 276p. bibliog.
Examines peasant uprisings and rural violence which occurred during the final seventy years of the Spanish empire in South America. The author focuses on regional rebellions which are viewed as being the result of local conditions and the abuse of natural rights in the areas of land holding, land usage and labour obligations.

101 **Economic decline and social change in an agrarian hinterland: Cochabamba (Bolivia) in the late colonial period.**
Brooke Larson. PhD dissertation, Columbia University, New York, 1978. 516p. bibliog.
An excellent study of the process of political and economic change in an agrarian hinterland of a mining enclave in 18th-century Bolivia. Despite signs of economic diversification and new forms of labour control that appeared in the region's economic evolution, Cochabamba did not experience the transition to nascent capitalist social relations. This dissertation tests the hypothesis that some regions of Latin America experienced economic diversification, growth, and transition to capitalism during a period of mineral decline and isolation from Spain.

102 **La estructura agraria del Alto Perú a fines del siglo XVIII: un análisis de tres regiones maiceras del partido de LareCaja en 1795.**
(The agrarian structure of Upper Peru at the end of the 18th century: an analysis of the three corn regions of the district of Lara Caja in 1795.)
Daniel Santamaría. *Desarrollo Económico*, vol. 18, no. 72 (1979), p. 579-95. map.
This essay is aimed primarily at historians who are interested in land tenure and land usage patterns in colonial Latin America. It forms part of an expanding scholarly bibliography focused on reconstructing the agrarian sector as fully as possible.

103 **Forced labor in colonial Peru.**
D. L. Wiedner. *(The) Americas* (Academy of American Franciscan History), vol. 16, no. 4 (April 1960), p. 357-83.
A study of the mita, or forced labour system, used by the Spanish at the silver mining complex in Potosí, Upper Peru.

104 **Hacienda and free community in eighteenth century Alto Peru (Upper Peru).**
Herbert S. Klein. *Journal of Latin American Studies*, vol. 7, no. 2 (1975), p. 193-220.
Examines the expansion and contraction of the hacienda and its relationship to free communities. During times of prosperity, haciendas would absorb, or attempt to absorb, Indian lands. During times of economic hardship, however, Indian communities grew at the expense of the haciendas.

105 **El mallku y la sociedad colonial en el siglo XVII: el caso de Jesús de Machaca.** (Native overlord and colonial society in the 17th century: the case of Jesús de Machaca.)
Silvia Rivera Cusicanqui. *Avances*, vol. 1, no. 1 (1978), p. 7-17. bibliog.
Examines the roles of tribal leaders and élites during the Spanish period, and considers how local élites became influential power brokers after the conquest. The author pays particular attention to the Kurakan, Jesús de Machaca.

106 **Migration and labor in seventeenth century Alto Perú (Bolivia).**
Ann L. Zulawski. PhD dissertation, Columbia University, New York, 1985. 345p. bibliog.
Examines how, and why, Oruro, a mining centre, and Pilayay Paspaya, an agricultural zone, developed Indian labour forces. This dissertation also studies the way in which migration affected Indian socio-economic patterns.

107 **Miners of the Red Mountain: Indian labor in Potosí, 1545-1650.**
Peter Bakewell. Albuquerque: University of New Mexico Press, 1984. 213p. bibliog.
This insightful study of the Potosí mining complex, and the native workers who made it function, focuses on the examination of the mita, or forced labour system. Bakewell shows that in the early years, Indians went to Potosí freely. Later, when mita service was introduced, free workers still constituted half of the labour force. This work is an excellent contribution to the economic history of Latin America.

108 **The mining society of Potosi, 1776-1810.**
Rose Marie Buechler. PhD dissertation, Syracuse University, New York, 1981. 431p. bibliog.
An extremely complete examination of the mining industry in the late colonial period. The study focuses on the Potosí mining guild, its composition, the origins of its members, the problems facing the mining industry, relations with the government and the 'stages passed through on the way to decadence'. Based on local (Potosí and Chuquisaca), viceregal (Buenos Aires), and imperial (Madrid and Seville) archival research.

109 **La mita de Potosí.** (The Potosí mita.)
Albert Crespo. *Revista Histórica* (Lima), vol. 22 (1955-56),
p. 169-82.

This is still the best short piece of interpretative writing on the Potosí mita, or forced labour system, introduced by Viceroy Francisco Toledo to solve labour shortages in the mines.

110 **Papeles de Cochabamba en el Archivo General de la Nación
Argentina.** (Documents on Cochabamba in the National Archive of Argentina.)
Eduardo Arze Quiroga. La Paz: Banco Hipotecario Nacional,
1975. 81p.

A calendar of papers from the periods 1762, 1786 and 1810-15 relating to the intendancy of Cochabamba, and housed in Buenos Aires.

111 **Pedro Chipana: cacique comerciante de Calamarca.** (Pedro Chipana: merchant-chief of Calamarca.)
Roberto Choque Canqui. *Avances*, vol. 1, no. 1 (1978),
p. 28-32. bibliog.

The study of indigenous political élites is of fundamental importance to Bolivian historiography as it helps to explain social and economic phenomena which occurred during the first fifty years of the Spanish era. During the 1530 to 1570 period traditional tribal leaders exercised wide ranging and fundamental economic power. The chiefs, such as Pedro Chipana were not simply instruments of the Spanish authorities. They promoted economic development and were engaged in a host of economic activities for personal gain, such as commerce, stockraising and real estate development and speculation.

112 **The Potosí mita, 1573-1700: compulsory Indian labor in the Andes.**
Jeffery A. Cole. Stanford, California: Stanford University Press,
1985. 206p. bibliog.

Examines the 17th-century mita, and how the Hapsburgs administered it. When peasants learned about working conditions at the Potosí mine, they attempted to escape obligatory service, some by moving away, but many more by attempting to purchase their freedom by paying a ransom. The second theme of this work is the Spanish administration of the mita. Based on archival research.

113 **The Potosí mita under Hapsburg administration. The seventeenth century.**
Jeffery A. Cole. PhD dissertation, University of Massachusetts,
Amherst, Massachusetts, 1981. 505p. bibliog.

A thorough examination of the Potosí mita in the 1600s. This study was researched from primary sources and is of particular relevance to the scholarly community.

114 **La propiedad de la tierra y la condición social del indio en el Alto Perú, 1780-1810.** (Landowning and the social condition of the Indian in Upper Peru, 1780-1810.)
Daniel Santamaría. *Desarrollo Económico*, vol. 17, no. 66 (1977), p. 253-66.
Examines the relationship of the free Indian community and the hacienda system during the final years of the Spanish empire in Bolivia.

115 **La rebelión de Juan Bustamante.** (The rebellion of Juan Bustamante.)
Emilio Vásquez. Lima: Librería Juan Mejía Baca, 1976. 408p. bibliog.
An historical account of a major Indian rebellion in the highland Andean region which took place in the late colonial period. This rebellion began a tradition of rebellion against the royal authorities in the 18th century.

116 **Registered silver production in the Potosí district, 1550-1735.**
Peter Bakewell. *Jahrbuch für Geschichte von Staat, Wirtschaft und Gesellschaft Lateinamerikas*, vol. 12 (1975), p. 67-103.
A data time series of the Spanish crown's share of mined silver from the Potosí mines. The data collected is used here to compute minimum production figures which are then presented as being indicators of long-range trends in production levels.

117 **The royal treasuries of the Spanish empire in America: Upper Peru and Bolivia.**
John J. TePaske, Herbert S. Klein. Durham, North Carolina: Duke University Press, 1982. 3 vols. bibliog.
Publishes the *cartas cuentas* (summaries of receipts and disbursements) of the royal treasuries of Peru (Volume 1); Upper Peru (Volume 2); and Chile and Río de la Plata (Volume 3).

118 **Rural rhythms of class conflict in eighteenth century Cochabamba.**
Brooke Larson. *Hispanic American Historical Review*, vol. 60, no. 3 (1980), p. 407-30.
Examines cycles of crisis, production and marketing together with their impact on relations between peasants and landlords.

119 **Silver production in the viceroyalty of Peru (1776-1824).**
John Fisher. *Hispanic American Historical Review*, vol. 55, no. 1 (1975), p. 25-44.
A systematic and thorough study of silver production during the final years of the colonial period. The study is based on extensive research of primary sources and will appeal to the serious student.

120 **Structure and profitability of royal finances in the viceroyalty of the Río de la Plata.**
Herbert S. Klein. *Hispanic American Historical Review*, vol. 53, no. 3 (1973), p. 440-69.

Studies the structure of royal income. Klein measures the revenue produced and investigates how it was spent.

121 **The structure of the hacendado class in late eighteenth century Alto Peru (Upper Peru).**
Herbert S. Klein. *Hispanic American Historical Review*, vol. 60, no. 2 (1980), p. 191-212. map.

Examines the class structure of Bolivia's colonial landed élite, and provides a preliminary estimate of its size, distribution, relative wealth and composition in the 18th-century province, or intendancy, of La Paz.

122 **Technical aid to Upper Peru: the Nordenflict Expedition.**
Rose Marie Buechler. *Journal of Latin American Studies*, vol. 5 (1973), p. 37-77.

An intricate and detailed study of technological advances presented to Spanish miners to improve productivity at the Potosí mining site.

123 **Technological change in Potosí: the silver boom of the 1570s.**
Peter Bakewell. *Jahrbuch für Geschichte von Staat, Wirtschaft und Gesellschaft Lateinamerikas*, vol. 14 (1977), p. 55-77. bibliog.

A thorough examination of the introduction of the patio process of refining silver by amalgamation and the impact of this technological advance on silver production at the Potosí site during the 16th century. The patio process is said here to have been more important to the revival of silver production in the area than was the mita, the system of forced labor.

# Independence and the 19th century

124 **The Antofagasta Company: a case study of peripheral capitalism.**
Thomas F. O'Brien. *Hispanic American Historical Review*, vol. 60, no. 1 (1980), p. 1-31.

Studies the operations of the Antofagasta Nitrate and Railway Company in the Pacific coast provinces of Peru and Bolivia during the last part of the 19th and early years of the 20th century. After William Gibbs, owner of the company, sold his interests in the firm in 1883, the operation was still dependent upon European capitalism and technology, even though it had become a Chilean enterprise.

125 **Attempted economic reform and innovation under Antonio de Sucre.**
William Lee Lofstrom. *Hispanic American Historical Review*, vol. 50, no. 2 (1970), p. 279-99.
Examines why Antonio José de Sucre's liberal reform package failed in Bolivia. Once Sucre had resigned as president, the Bolivian élites, who had always regarded him as an interfering outsider, returned to their traditional practices.

126 **Cartas inéditas del Gran Mariscal Santa Cruz al General Nieto sobre los preparativos de la primera expedición restauradora.**
(Unpublished letters of Grand Marshal Santa Cruz to General Nieto about the preparations for the first restorative expedition.)
Félix Denegri Luna. *Boletín del Instituto Riva-Aguero*, vol. 10 (1975-76), p. 9-26.
General Santa Cruz appreciated the importance of naval power in the Peru–Bolivia Confederation's war with Chile. However, he did not trust the navy because its officers had supported a late enemy of his. He, therefore, placed trusted army officers in command of naval vessels even though they were not trained in naval warfare.

127 **Damasco de Uriburu, a mining entrepreneur in early nineteenth-century Bolivia.**
William Lee Lofstrom. *Special Studies* (State University of New York at Buffalo), vol. 35 (1973). 66p. bibliog.
Damasco de Uriburu was not an important man. Some might consider him a failure. However, he lived and worked during an important period of regional development and was intimately involved in the silver mining industry of the new born Republic of Bolivia. A Spanish version is available, entitled *Damasco de Uriburu, un empresario minero de principios del siglo XIX en Bolivia* (La Paz: Editorial los Amigos del Libro, 1982. 101p. Biblioteca Minera Boliviana Series).

128 **Dos visiones de la relación ayllu/estado: la resistencia de los indios de Chayanta a la revisita general (1882-1885).** (Two views of community/state relations: the resistance of the Chayanta Indians to the general census, 1882-1885.)
Tristan Platt. *Historia Boliviana*, vol. 2 (1982), p. 33-46. bibliog.
An examination of the liberal ideology associated with the general census is contrasted with the Indian conception of mutual obligations between village and state.

129 **Eagles of the Andes: South American struggles for independence.**
Carleton Beals. New York: Chilton Books, 1963. 363p. maps.
A popular, readable book for a general audience, which surveys the wars of independence in Spanish South America. A discussion of Simón Bolívar's Bolivian campaigns is included.

130 **The economic and social structure of silver mining in XIX century Bolivia.**
Antonio Mitre. PhD dissertation, Columbia University, New York, 1978. 317p. bibliog.
Focuses on the evolution of the silver mining industry in the 19th century and charts the external and internal influences on its expansions and contractions.

131 **The emergence of the Republic of Bolivia.**
Charles Arnade. Gainesville, Florida: University of Florida Press, 1957. 269p. map. bibliog.
A first attempt to present to the English-reading audience the history of the Bolivian Independence movement. This is a concise and readable monograph, which not only chronicles the events of Bolivian Independence but also probes the national character.

132 **The emergence of the tin industry in Bolivia.**
J. Hillman. *Journal of Latin American Studies*, vol. 16, no. 2 (Nov. 1984), p. 403-37.
A scholarly examination of the development of the tin industry in Bolivia in the 19th century, based on primary research. Hillman looks at it from a global perspective, first, and then traces the emergent industry.

133 **Gabriel Rene-Moreno and the intellectual context of late nineteenth-century South America.**
Gertrude M. Yeager. *Social Science Quarterly*, vol. 59, no. 1 (1978), p. 77-92.
Studies the life and intellectual development of the doyen of Bolivian history, Gabriel Rene-Moreno, who lived his entire life outside Bolivia and participated actively in the intellectual community which existed in southern South America. His relationship to other South American thinkers is also discussed, together with his place in the context of Bolivian letters.

134 **General Francis Burdett O'Connor.**
Eric Lambert. *Irish Sword*, vol. 13, no. 15 (1977), p. 128-33.
A biography of Francis O'Connor (1791-1871) who served as an officer with the liberation forces of Simón Bolívar in the Upper Peru campaigns.

135 **Historia de Bolivia.** (History of Bolivia.)
Alcides Arguedas. La Paz: Librería y Editorial 'Juventud', 1981. 5 vols. bibliog.
A very good history of Bolivia by a noted intellectual. It traces Bolivian history from Independence (1825), to the 1880s. Each volume is well written and enjoyable to read, and each is written so as to stand independently of the others. The volumes are entitled: 1. 'The foundation of the Republic'; 2. the 'Educated caudillos'; 3. 'Dictatorship and anarchy'; 4. 'People in action'; and 5. the 'Barbaric caudillos'.

136 **The impact of the crisis of nineteenth-century mining on regional economies: the example of the Bolivian Yungas, 1786-1838.**
Herbert S. Klein.   In: *Social fabric and spatial structure in colonial Latin America.* Edited by D. Robinson. Ann Arbor, Michigan: University Microfilms, 1975, p. 315-38.
This essay utilizes census data to establish the impact of mining cycles in Potosí on the population and on coca production in the Yungas region of Bolivia.

137 **Original accumulation, capitalism, and pre-capitalistic agriculture in Bolivia (1870-1885).**
Gustavo Rodríguez O.   *Latin American Perspectives*, vol. 7, no. 4 (1980), p. 50-66.
Three central problems have been ignored by Bolivian historians to date: the origins of capitalism in Bolivia; the reason for capitalism's inability to destroy completely the pre-capitalistic order; and the pre-capitalistic modes in the 19th century. A set of hypotheses to study these questions is presented here.

138 **Participación popular en la independencia de Bolivia.** (Popular participation in Bolivian Independence.)
René Arze Aguirre.   La Paz: Editorial Don Bosco, 1979. 271p. maps. bibliog.
A prize-winning monograph and the first scholarly attempt to document popular, or lower-class, participation in the campaigns for Bolivian Independence. This study, which is based on extensive documentation and which is quite readable, argues that lower-class participation was both extensive and important during the first phase of the Independence movement, but that this participation was limited to the early years.

139 **Peasant response to the market and the land question in 18th and 19th century Bolivia.**
Herbert S. Klein.   *Nova Americana*, no. 5 (1982), p. 103-33, maps. bibliog.
Argues that Indian communities retained a strong presence in Bolivia until the 1880s. Tribute rolls suggest that communities grew to the 1890s, at which time they were repressed by the government.

140 **The politics of the Bolivian army: institutional development [1879] to 1935.**
James Dunkerley.   PhD dissertation, Oxford University, Oxford, England, 1979. 307p. maps. bibliog.
Examines the development of the modern Bolivian army during the crucial period between the War of the Pacific and the Chaco War.

141 **The promise and problem of reform: attempted social and economic change in the first years of Bolivian Independence.**
William Lee Lofstrom. Ithaca, New York: Cornell University Press, 1972. 626p. bibliog.

A scholarly monograph which examines the administration of Antonio José de Sucre, first president of Bolivia (1825-28). This lengthy work may very well be the definitive study of the attempted social and economic reform of the Sucre presidency. It demonstrates why the reforms were largely unsuccessful. Although these reforms failed the Bolivian example does provide a necessary case-study of the reform effort. This work has also been published in Spanish as *El Mariscal Sucre en Bolivia: la promesa y el problema de la reforma: el intento de cambio económico y social en los primeros años de la independencia boliviana* (La Paz: Editorial 'e Impr. Alenkar', 1983. 586p.).

142 **South American power politics during the 1820s.**
Ronald L. Seckinger. *Hispanic American Historical Review*, vol. 56, no. 2 (1976), p. 241-67.

Analyses the relations between the South American republics and the Brazilian empire in the immediate aftermath of Independence. Because of its Portuguese heritage, Brazil aroused suspicion among the Hispanic American nations as did Simón Bolívar's attempts to forge a powerful Andean federation. Attempts to develop strong ties among the principal nations of South America failed because of this tradition of fear.

143 **Sub-regional integration in nineteenth-century South America: Andrés Santa Cruz and the Peru–Bolivian Confederation, 1835-1839.**
Philip Parkerson. PhD dissertation, University of Florida, Gainesville, Florida, 1979. 384p. bibliog.

Examines the attempts of Andrés Santa Cruz (1792-1865) to unite the lower and upper sections of Peru into a single nation state during the early 19th century.

144 **Survival of Indian communities in nineteenth-century Bolivia: a regional comparison.**
Edwin P. Grieshaber. *Journal of Latin American Studies*, vol. 12, no. 2 (1980), p. 223-68.

Despite the expansion of the hacienda system in Bolivia during the 19th-century, Indian communities survived in many parts of South America. This article examines how, and why, these Indian communities continued to exist. See also the author's *Survival of Indian communities in nineteenth-century Bolivia* (PhD dissertation, University of North Carolina, Chapel Hill, 1977. 308p. maps. bibliog.).

# Modern period (20th century)

### 145 Banzer's Bolivia.
Laurence Whitehead. *Current History*, vol. 70, no. 413 (1976), p. 61-64.

General Hugo Banzer tried to win favour through economic and territorial negotiations with Chile, mainly to gain a seaport, but his régime had little to bargain with.

### 146 Beyond the revolution; Bolivia since 1952.
Edited by James M. Malloy, Richard Thorn. Pittsburgh, Pennsylvania: University of Pittsburgh Press, 1971. 402p. maps. bibliog.

This excellent series of essays addressing changing conditions in Bolivian society, politics and the economy since the 1952 revolution was presented at an interdisciplinary seminar sponsored by the University of Pittsburgh in 1966. Essays include: Herbert S. Klein's 'Prelude to the revolution'; James M. Malloy's 'Revolutionary politics'; and James W. Wilkie's 'Public expenditure since 1952'.

### 147 Bolivia and its social literature before and after the Chaco War: a historical study of social and literary revolution.
Murdo MacLeod. PhD dissertation, University of Florida, Gainesville, Florida, 1962. 254p. bibliog.

The Chaco War, (1932-35), one of the many causes of the 1952 revolution, also created an intellectual revolution in Bolivia. The young writers of the Chaco generation had three general aims: to discover and explain the nature of Bolivian society; to seek and support the campaigns for social justice; and lastly, to develop in Bolivia an independent culture.

### 148 Bolivia: Andean power shift.
James Kohl. *Progressive*, vol. 41, no. 2 (1977), p. 39-42.

Recent studies show that between 1962 and 1971, the year in which Hugo Banzer came to power, the production of agricultural crops such as cotton, coffee and sugar rose by more than eight hundred per cent. The economic development of the eastern areas of Bolivia has been spectacular. Kohl concludes that revolutions are often only the political expression of new economic realities.

### 149 Bolivia in 1956: an analysis of political and economic events.
Lois D. Martin. Stanford, California: Stanford University Press, 1958, 46p. bibliog. (Hispanic American Studies).

A brief analysis of the 1952 revolution's impact on Bolivian political culture and economic development.

150 **Bolivia moves toward democracy.**
Waltraud Queiser Morales. *Current History*, vol. 78, no. 454
(1980), p. 76-79, 86-88.

Analyses electoral practices and the reasons for a series of unstable military
régimes in the 1970s. Morales sees the root of the problem as being economic in
nature.

151 **Bolivia, press and revolution 1932-1964.**
Jerry A. Knudson. New York: University Press of America,
1986. 488p.

Examines the role of the press in the MNR (Movimiento Nacionalista
Revolucionario) revolution, and argues that the press was a vehicle for social
change because there was no other means for the circulation of ideas. This is also
a history of modern journalism in Bolivia and, in particular, a history of the
creation of the first mass-based newspaper, *El Universal*, which served as a
training ground for a generation of writers. While the study focuses on *El
Universal*, it also pays attention to smaller, more specialized, newspapers, such as
*La Calle, La Marcha, La Nación, La Tarde* and *Presencia*, among others.

152 **The Bolivian coup of 1964: a sociological analysis.**
J. Calderón. Buffalo, New York: Council on International
Studies, 1972. 137p. bibliog.

Focuses on Bolivian society and on major developments between 1952 and the
1964 coup which ousted the MNR (Movimiento Nacionalista Revolucionario)
from office. A good part of the emphasis is placed on the consequences of
dependence in Third World areas, the resistance to the revolution and the
circumstances surrounding the coup itself.

153 **The Bolivian military in politics.**
Joseph D. Stafford. *Secolas*, vol. 10 (1979), p. 81-94.

Applies three models of political behaviour to Bolivian politics in the period 1968
to 1974. The models included are clientelism, corporatism and militarism.
Militarism is judged to be the strategy which best explains political behaviour in
Bolivia during this period.

154 **The Bolivian national revolution.**
Robert J. Alexander. New Brunswick, New Jersey: Rutgers
University Press, 1958. 302p. bibliog.

A somewhat dated but objective analysis of the MNR revolution of 1952. The
MNR (Movimiento Nacionalista Revolucionario) is seen as a democratic political
movement which desired to bring Bolivia into the 20th century. US liberals were
urged to defend it and to advocate the extension of the credits necessary to keep
the experiment afloat.

155  **The Bolivian revolution and U.S. aid since 1952; financial**
     **background and context of political decisions.**
     James W. Wilkie.   Los Angeles, California: Latin American
     Center, University of California, 1969. 98p. bibliog.

Social and economic statistics are used to examine Bolivia's political problems of
development. Per capita growth and budgetary policy are seen as tests of
ideology. Wilkie concludes that, in the budgetary sense, post-1952 Bolivia is not
revolutionary as State policy meshed nicely with the patterns of expenditure
established in 1945. Throughout this work he develops the thesis that, if national
planners are not aware of the financial factors that influence them, there is little
possibility that they can effectively manipulate their environment to achieve
political stability.

156  **Bolivia's MNR: a study of a national popular movement in Latin**
     **America.**
     James M. Malloy.   Buffalo, New York: Council on International
     Studies, 1971. 55p. bibliog.

A now classic work, aimed at students, which examines the MNR movement and
contemporary Bolivian political culture. The author is a respected expert in this
field and is frustrated with Bolivia's inability to achieve change.

157  **Bolivia's popular assembly of 1971 and the overthrow of General**
     **Juan José Torres.**
     Buffalo, New York: Council on International Studies, 1974. 70p.

The fate of the ten-month-old Torres régime posed more questions than it
answered. Torres' radicalism, and the fever of slogans it produced, merely
exacerbated an already volatile situation and sent Bolivia reeling into one of the
most repressive régimes in contemporary Latin America; that of Hugo Banzer.
The Torres experiment only muddied the political waters of Bolivia; it had no
positive impact.

158  **Bolivia's social revolution, 1952-1959.**
     Charles Arnade.   *Journal of Interamerican Studies and World*
     *Affairs*, vol. 1, no. 3 (1959), p. 341-52.

A sympathetic examination of the first period of the MNR (Movimiento
Nacionalista Revolucionario) in power.

159  **The Chaco War.**
     A. J. English.   *Army Quarterly and Defence Journal*, vol. 109,
     no. 3 (1979), p. 350-58.

Examines the military campaigns of the Chaco War (1932-35).

160 **Che Guevara on revolution; a documentary overview.**
Ernesto Guevara.   Coral Gables, Florida: University of Miami
Press, 1969. 255p. bibliog.

A collection of Che Guevara's writings on revolution in the developing world
which infer that domestic and foreign constraints have shaped revolutions, and
not government policies *per se*.

161 **Che's Bolivian adventure.**
John Waghelstein.   *Military Review*, vol. 59, no. 8 (1979),
p. 39-48.

Reviews the reasons why Che Guevara's Bolivian campaign failed. Included
among the military errors were weaknesses in the supply system, a lack of
intelligence, and flawed communication networks. Guevara's political errors
included his personalistic domination of the movement and his refusal to
collaborate with Bolivian revolutionary groups, such as the Communist Party.

162 **Che's guerrilla war.**
Regis Debray, translated by Rosemary Sheed.   Harmondsworth,
England: Penguin, 1975. 156p.

Analyses the failure of Che Guevara's foco strategy in Bolivia which held that a
small band of revolutionaries could begin a revolution, succeed, and then co-opt
the leadership of the Communist Party. This study is based on Debray's own
observations and participation in the campaign.

163 **The Ciza and Ucureña War: syndical violence and national
revolution in Bolivia.**
James V. Kohl.   *Hispanic American Historical Review*, vol. 62,
no. 4 (1982), p. 607-28.

Concentrates on the patronage system as it developed in rural Cochabamba
during the 1952 revolution, and the political infighting in the *sindicato*, or union
movement, of the national revolution. Explores the highpoint of union power in
rural areas, the nature of the power élites, and the ties between rural peasant
leadership and the national movement.

164 **Class, union, party: the development of the revolutionary union
movement in Bolivia, 1905-1952.**
Steven S. Volk.   *Science and Society*, vol. 39, no. 1 (1975),
p. 26-43; vol. 39, no. 2, p. 180-98.

Labour unions provided the revolutionary thrust in the development of Bolivian
national political movements. The political organization of the labour movement
became important only with the end of the Chaco War in 1935. Prior to this date
the unions had fought for economic and political rights.

165 **The complete Bolivian diaries of Che Guevara and other
 captured documents.**
 Compiled by James Deniel. New York: Stein & Day, 1968. 330p.
 maps.

The purpose of Guevara's expedition to Bolivia in 1966 was to create sufficient
turmoil to warrant US military intervention. Che had hoped to create another
Vietnam. US intervention, he believed, would serve as a catalyst for revolutionary movements throughout South America.

166 **The conduct of the Chaco War.**
 David Zook. New Haven, Connecticut: Bookman Associates,
 1960. 331p. map. bibliog.

Discusses the political, economic and military aspects of the Chaco War fought
between Bolivia and Paraguay, 1932-35. One of the best, and one of the first,
books written on this war in any language.

167 **The crisis of legitimacy and the origins of social revolution.**
 Herbert S. Klein. *Journal of Interamerican Studies and World
 Affairs*, vol. 10, no. 1 (1968), p. 108-16.

Studies the causes of the MNR revolution with particular attention to the impact
of the Chaco War and the political crisis which arose from Bolivia's defeat at the
hands of Paraguay.

168 **The diary of Che Guevara, Bolivia: November 7 1966-October 7
 1967. The authorized text in English and Spanish. Introduction by
 Fidel Castro.**
 Ernesto Guevara. New York: Bantam Books, 1968. 191p. map.

The first English translation of Che's Bolivian diary.

169 **Documentos para una historia de la guerra del Chaco.** (Documents
 for a history of the Chaco War.)
 Cochabamba, Bolivia: Editorial Universitaria, Universidad
 Boliviana Mayor de 'San Simón', 1974. 455p.

Includes documents from the Chaco War, together with a brief chapter by
Demetrio Canelos on the government of Daniel Salamanca.

170 **Egalitarian reformism in the Third World vs. the military: a profile
 of failure.**
 Miles D. Wolpin. *Journal of Peace Research*, vol. 15, no. 2
 (1978), p. 89-101.

Traces the patterns of civilian–military relations associated with ten deposed
reformist administrations including the Torres régime of Bolivia (1971). The
author also examines the origins and composition of the anti-reformist coalitions
and the overt and covert actions of the US government in toppling reformist
régimes.

35

171 **La experiencia de los partidos socialistas (período 1914-1934).** (The experience of the Socialist parties [1914-34 period.])
Myrna Pacello. La Paz: *Temas Sociales* (June 1971), p. 74-83.

Discusses the early years of Bolivia's Socialist and Communist parties and considers why they failed to achieve power in the era prior to the appearance of the MNR movement.

172 **From national populism to national corporatism: the case of Bolivia: 1952-1970.**
Melvin Burke, James M. Malloy. *Studies in Comparative International Development*, vol. 9, no. 1 (1974), p. 49-73.

Traces the developments in Bolivia during this period which turned a populist revolutionary government into a military régime. Political factionalism so weakened the parties that they turned to the military for support and opened the door for a *golpe de estado*.

173 **Germán Busch and the era of 'military socialism' in Bolivia.**
Herbert S. Klein. *Hispanic American Historical Review*, vol. 47, no. 2 (1967), p. 166-84.

Under the leadership of David Toro and Germán Busch the traditional intra-class political system of Bolivia was destroyed. This paved the way for a radical restructuring of national political life and ultimately created the conditions for the 1952 revolution. See also Klein's 'David Toro and the establishment of military socialism' (q.v.).

174 **David Toro and the establishment of military socialism.**
Herbert S. Klein. *Hispanic American Historical Review*, vol. 45, no. 1 (1965), p. 25-62.

Under the régimes of David Toro and Germán Busch Bolivia's traditional political party system was destroyed and the way was prepared for a new revolutionary ideology and the eventual success of the 1952 revolution.

175 **Einige Gedanken zum Faschismus im heutigen Lateinamerika.**
(Some reflections on Fascism in present-day Latin America.)
Rodmy Arismendi. *Einheit* (GDR), vol. 32, no. 2 (1977), p. 211-19.

The co-operation of the local oligarchies of Chile, Guatemala, Brazil, Bolivia and Uruguay with US military and economic interest groups strengthened Fascist tendencies in these societies during the 1960s and 1970s.

176 **The influence of Henri Barbusse in Bolivia.**
Peter J. Gold. *Bulletin of Latin American Research* (Oxford), vol. 2, no. 2 (May 1983), p. 117-22. bibliog.

Examines the literary and political influence of the French Communist writer and intellectual Henri Barbusse in Bolivia in the 1930s and 1940s. His novel *Le feu*

(The fire) was a model for the Chaco War novel. His ideas were introduced into Bolivia by José Carlos Mariatequs.

177 **Insurgency and counterinsurgency in Latin America, 1960-1980.**
Richard Weitz. *Political Science Quarterly*, vol. 101, no. 3 (1986), p. 397-413.

Weitz calls for the re-examination of previous guerrilla operations in Latin America in the light of current events in El Salvador, Colombia, Guatemala and Peru. To shed further light on this problem, four earlier revolutions are studied, two of which succeeded (Cuba and Nicaragua), and two of which failed (Venezuela, and Bolivia, in 1967).

178 **Klaus Barbie: the butcher of Lyons.**
Tom Bower. New York: Pantheon, 1984. 248p.

A popular biography of this infamous Nazi war criminal.

179 **Labor strikes and reciprocity on Chuquisaca haciendas.**
Erick Detlef Langer. *Hispanic American Historical Review*, vol. 65, no. 2 (1985), p. 255-77.

Culture played an essential role in the resistance of hacienda peons (day-labourers) to changes in employment and working conditions. Any change made peasants feel threatened as they perceived a loss of rights and privileges. This resulted in a number of strikes.

180 **The last of Bolivia's MNR?**
Richard W. Patch. Hanover, New Hampshire: American Universities Field Staff, 1964. 25p. (West Coast South America Series, vol. 9, no. 5).

Important lessons can be drawn from the Bolivian situation of 1964. The author considers the question: How can the United States achieve a goal of self-sustaining economic development, in a country such as Bolivia (which many people think is conducive to political stability), without becoming deeply involved in the planning process? Patch also notes that the U S role in Bolivia is so great that many Bolivians assign responsibility for its national future to the United States.

181 **The Latin American military as a socio-political force: case studies of Bolivia and Argentina.**
Charles Corbett. Coral Gables, Florida: Center for Advanced International Studies, University of Miami, 1972. 143p. bibliog.

Compares and contrasts the political role of the military in Bolivia and Argentina. The analysis combines an evaluation of professionalism, a consideration of the formation of political élites, and an examination of security doctrines. Also included is an historical review of the military's participation in 20th-century coups.

37

182 **The legacy of populism in Bolivia: from the MNR to military rule.**
Christopher Mitchell. New York: Praeger, 1977. 167p. bibliog.
This is the first serious attempt to study the nature of the MNR movement. The party, made up of heterogeneous forces, but dominated by the middle classes, became conservative once it attained power. Old problems such as conflict between the MNR and the military, and conflict among various political groups created tensions and maintained obstacles to political stability.

183 **The life and career of Klaus Barbie: an eyewitness record.**
John Beattie. London: Methuen, 1984. 228p.
A biography of Klaus Barbie who was smuggled out of France and into Bolivia by the US government.

184 **The massacre in the Cochabamba valley: Bolivian police over-react and kill 100 citizens.**
LADOC, vol. 52 (Nov. 1974), p. 1-11.
A descriptive account of an unfortunate confrontation in late January, 1974, between the Hugo Banzer régime, and a group of peasants, who rebelled because of sharp increases in the price of food. The report is based on information gathered by the Bolivian Commission for Justice and Peace. The Commission conducted interviews with seventy persons, including thirty peasants (six of them peasant leaders), eight officials (military and civilian), three journalists, two doctors and twelve priests.

185 **Military intervention in Bolivia: the overthrow of Paz Estenssoro and the MNR.**
William M. Brill. Washington, DC: Institute for the Comparative Study of Political Systems, 1967. 68p. bibliog.
Studies why the military, an institution which had been reformed by Paz, participated in his removal from power.

186 **Miners as voters: the electoral process in Bolivia's mining camps.**
Laurence Whitehead. *Journal of Latin American Studies*, vol. 13, no. 2 (Nov. 1981), p. 313-46. bibliog.
An examination of the politicization of Bolivian miners prior to the MNR revolution of 1952. The 1940 elections were the key to turning miners into political activists and Victor Paz Estenssoro was significant in bringing them into the MNR fold.

187 **The MNR Party and the Villarroel administration: 1943-1946.**
Joseph Holtey. PhD dissertation, Arizona State University, Tempe, Arizona, 1980. 270p. bibliog.
In December of 1943 the MNR, together with a small military contingent, installed Gualberto Villarroel as head of the government. This administration failed to provide political stability to Bolivia partly because the United States refused to grant recognition.

188 **National-popular state, state capitalism and military dictatorship in Bolivia, 1952-1975.**
René A. Mayorga. *Latin American Perspectives*, vol.5, no. 2 (spring 1978), p. 89-119.
This interpretative essay, based on both primary and secondary sources, concludes that although the 1952 revolution was an armed proletarian uprising, it resulted in a bourgeois economic and political order.

189 **National revolution to revolution of restoration – arms and factional politics in Bolivia.**
J. V. Kohl. *Inter-American Economic Affairs*, vol. 39, no. 1 (1985), p. 3-30.
Examines the middle years of the MNR revolution.

190 **The Nazi octopus in South America.**
Hugo Fernández Artucio. London: Robert Hale, 1943. 311p.
A personal history and account of the spread of Fascism through South America, including Bolivia. This is a classic piece of Second World War literature.

191 **Observations on student activism in Bolivia.**
Leonard Cardenas, Jr. *Journal of Sociology*, vol. 2, no. 1 (1971), p. 34-45.
A study of the political behaviour and attitudes of Bolivian university students. In Bolivia even the movement for Independence at the beginning of the 19th century began in a university. This tradition has continued into this century and, since the 1930s, the orientation of the university curriculum has been Marxist. Frequently, university students provide the fuse for manifestations of popular discontent.

192 **Oral history projects in Argentina, Chile, Peru, and Bolivia.**
Peter J. Sehlinger. *International Journal of Oral History*, vol. 5, no. 3 (1984) p. 168-73.
Reviews oral history projects in Bolivia between 1954 and 1984, outlining where they took place and assessing their usefulness.

193 **Parties and political change in Bolivia 1880-1952.**
Herbert S. Klein. London: Cambridge University Press, 1962. 451p. bibliog.
The best available study in English of the political culture and the political system which existed in Bolivia in the fifty years before the MNR revolution. Studies the nature of intra-class political rivalries, the party structure, and the ideological considerations and position of the national and regional élites of Bolivia.

194 **Peasant and revolution in Bolivia, April 1, 1952 – August 2, 1952.**
James V. Kohl. *Hispanic American Historical Review*, vol. 58,
no. 2 (1978), p. 238-59.

The MNR revolution of 1952 was essentially an urban revolution. The struggle,
however, developed an agrarian dimension and this resulted in the land reform
decrees of August 1953.

195 **Politics of the Chaco Peace Conference 1935-1939.**
Leslie B. Rout, Jr. Austin, Texas; London: University of Texas
Press, 1970. 268p. 9 maps. bibliog. (Latin American Monograph,
no. 19).

Examines the three major aspects of the Chaco dispute which led to war between
Bolivia and Paraguay and the inter-American Peace Conference which settled it.
Agreements were achieved in total secrecy. This text is based on extensive
primary documentation from Brazilian, Argentine, Uruguayan and Bolivian
archives.

196 **The pro and anti-Castristas in La Paz.**
Richard W. Patch. Hanover, New Hampshire: American
Universities Field Staff, 1962. 6p. (West Coast South America
Series, vol. 9, no. 2).

It is commonly believed that sympathy for Fidel Castro in Bolivia is weak. This is
an eyewitness account of a pro-Castro demonstration which turned into a political
riot in La Paz.

197 **Rebellion in the veins: political struggle in Bolivia, 1952-82.**
James Dunkerley. London: Verso, 1984. 385p.

Describes a rich period in Bolivian development and the four major actors in
Bolivia's contemporary drama: the MNR, the tin miners, the military and the
United States. The work is strongest in its explanation of the details of MNR
politics and the role of the United States. This work is solid and offers useful
insights into Bolivian political evolution. Photographs and tables are also
included.

198 **The (revolucíon nacional) and the MNR in Bolivia.**
William Stokes. *Inter-American Economic Affairs*, vol. 12, no. 4
(1959), p. 28-51.

A lengthy critique of the MNR policies. The author also questions the raison
d'être of a US policy which supports a régime strongly influenced by Marxist
ideology.

199 **Rural society and land consolidation in a declining economy: Chuquisaca, Bolivia 1880-1930.**
Erick Detlef Langer.   PhD dissertation, Stanford University, Stanford, California, 1984. 338p. maps. bibliog.

This study examines the impact of the late 19th-century rise and 20th-century decline of the Potosí silver mining economy on the rural society of the department of Chuquisaca. Land tenure and labour conditions are studied in the four provinces of that department.

200 **El sesquicentenario de la independencia de Bolivia.** (The 150th anniversary of Bolivian Independence.)
Omar Roca.   *Casa de las Américas* (Cuba), vol. 16, no. 94 (1976), p. 92-103.

This survey of Bolivian revolutions from Independence to the present day focuses on the struggle of the peasantry against the aristocratic and middle classes. The 20th-century revolutions have revealed the growing power of the working classes in achieving their rights, although they suffered a setback with the arrival of the Banzer government.

201 **Shock of recognition: the Bolivian press views the Mexican and Cuban revolutions.**
Jerry A. Knudson.   *Proceedings of the Pacific Coast Council on Latin American Studies*, vol. 9 (1982), p. 83-90.

A sketch of Bolivian reaction to the Cárdenas era and the first four years of Castro's Cuban Revolution.

202 **Social mobility and economic development: the vital parameters of the Bolivian revolution.**
C. F. Bergsten.   *Journal of Interamerican Studies and World Affairs*, vol. 6, no. 3 (1964), p. 367-76.

Explores the social and economic reforms suggested by the MNR. The emphasis was on promoting nationalization of the tin industry, and introducing universal suffrage, agrarian reform and public primary education.

203 **The state in an enclave economy: political instability in Bolivia 1900-1952.**
Carmenza Gallo.   PhD dissertation, Boston University, Boston, Massachusetts, 1985. 204p.

Develops a framework in which to study political instability. Bolivian history suggests that instability resulted from: (1) low demand for public goods; (2) a lack of demand for the state to develop institutions able to organize power; and (3) the undermining of the state apparatus due to its heavy dependence on tin exports.

204 **10 años de revolución, 1952-1962.** (Ten years of revolution, 1952-62.)
La Paz: Dirección Nacional de Informaciones, 1962. 263p.

An important piece of government propaganda recounting the 1952 revolution and its beneficial results.

205 **The tragedy of Bolivia: a people crucified.**
Alberto Ostria Gutiérrez, translated by E. Golden. New York: Devin-Adair Co., 1958. 224p.

Presents a sweeping and personal vision of Bolivia during the difficult years between 1943 and 1952. The victory of the MNR in 1952 was not a national victory but a tragedy. It brought destruction to the entire society; no institution was spared, and terrorism became a part of political life. The only real winner in this tragic event was Moscow.

206 **Varieties of Latin American revolutions and rebellions.**
Paul Herrick, Robert S. Robins. *Journal of Developing Areas,* vol. 10, no. 3 (1976), p. 317-36.

Revolutions and rebellions in Latin America are classified and analysed in a typology which covers total revolution (Mexico, 1910), political revolution (Brazil, 1964), and policy rebellion (Venezuela, 1948). This study cites examples from Bolivian history.

207 **The workers' movement and the Bolivian revolution reconsidered.**
Paul Cammack. *Politics and Society,* vol. 11, no. 2 (1982), p. 211-22.

Examines how international and national events contributed to a decrease in political power for the tin miners.

208 **The workers' revolution and the Bolivian revolution reconsidered – reply.**
B. Useem. *Politics and Society,* vol. 11, no. 2 (1982), p. 223-29.

Explains why labour, which had lost power after the MNR revolution, became institutionalized.

# Politics

**209  An aborted democracy.**
Dennis Devine.  *Worldview*, vol. 24 (1981), p. 19-20.
Argues that the coup of July 1980 in Bolivia was different from the nation's other 188 military interventions.

**210  Authoritarianism and corporatism: the case of Bolivia.**
James M. Malloy.  In: *Authoritarianism and corporatism in Latin America*. Edited by James M. Malloy. Pittsburgh, Pennsylvania: University of Pittsburgh Press, 1977, p. 459-88.
Examines the political institutions of contemporary Bolivia in the light of new social science thinking concerning the concepts of 'authoritarianism and corporatism' in Latin American politics.

**211  Bolivia: coup d'état.**
James Dunkerley.  London: Latin America Bureau, 1980. 88p.
map.
On 17 July, 1980, Bolivia suffered the most bloody coup of its history. The goal of General Gustavo García Meza was to do away with all opposition. This included progressive clergy, trade unionists, and peasant organizers. García Meza envisaged the establishment of a right-wing régime similar to that in Chile.

**212  Bolivia: election or another coup?**
Vadim Listov.  *New Times* (Moscow), vol. 20 (May 1980), p. 26-27.
Discusses briefly the political options Bolivia might use in order to solve its continual political instability.

213 **Bolivia, hacia la democracia: apuntes histórico-políticos.** (Bolivia, towards democracy: historical-political notes.)
Walter Ríos Gamboa. La Paz: Khana Cruz, 1980. 179p. bibliog.
Traces Bolivia's tortured and twisted route to democracy with an emphasis on current political crises.

214 **Bolivia, 1980-1981: the political system in crisis.**
James Dunkerley. London: Institute of Latin American Studies, University of London, 1982. 48p. (Working Papers, 8).
An article-length description of the collapse of the election process in Bolivia. The crisis stemmed from the inability of any of the political parties to overcome sectarianism and put forward a coherent political solution. This sectarianism has its roots in Bolivia's parliamentary tradition and the ambiguous legacy of the populist MNR movement.

215 **Bolivia: past, present, and future of its politics.**
Robert J. Alexander. New York: Praeger, 1982. 157p.
A popular analytical political history of Bolivia by a noted scholar, which emphasizes the post-Chaco War era. A good introduction to contemporary Bolivia.

216 **Bolivia, the sad and corrupt end of the revolution.**
James M. Malloy. Hanover, New Hampshire: Universities Field Staff International (UFSI), 1982. 9p.
A pessimistic review of Bolivian political culture in the aftermath of Banzer. Like Dunkerley in *Bolivia, 1980-1981: the political system in crisis* (q.v.), Malloy discusses the political weaknesses present in Bolivia and the rotation of power between military governments and weak democracies.

217 **Bolivia's democratic experiment.**
Robert J. Alexander. *Current History*, vol. 84, no. 499 (1985), p. 73-76.
The inauguration of President Hernán Siles Zuazo in 1982 was an advance for democracy, but a democratic republic has not yet been established. Problems in Bolivia are almost without solution and include the incorporation of the Indian into the society, the development of agriculture and general economic expansion and modernization.

218 **Bolivia's failed democratization of 1977-1980.**
Laurence Whitehead. Washington, DC: Wilson Center, Paper 100 (1981). 24p.
Examines how economic, international and political problems brought about a return to military rule. Also provides a good chronology of political events during a complex period.

219 **Bolivia's national revolution thirty years later: success or failure?**
Waltraud Queiser Morales. *Secolas*, vol. 15 (1984), p. 5-34.
An overview of the MNR's ability to introduce meaningful change into Bolivian society. Concludes that Bolivia did have a revolution and its successes have been no less impressive than those of Mexico or Cuba.

220 **Democracia y golpe militar.** (Democracy and military takeover.)
Alfredo Peña. Caracas, Venezuela: Editorial Ateneo de Caracas, 1979. 292p.
A series of interviews with seven Latin American ex-presidents, conducted in March 1979 by Alfredo Peña, a Venezuelan journalist. Included here is an interview with Hernán Siles Zuazo.

221 **Documentos políticos de Bolivia.** (Bolivian political documents.)
Guillermo Lora. La Paz: Editorial los Amigos del Libro, 1970. 606p.
Gives information concerning political parties in the 1960s in Bolivia and their programmes.

222 **Does Fascism exist in Latin America.**
José Soares. *World Marxist Review*, vol. 19, no. 12 (1976), p. 79-86.
Discusses whether or not right-wing régimes in Latin America in the mid-1970s were truly Fascist in nature. Examples from modern Bolivian history are included.

223 **The domestic and international politics of internal conflict: a comparative analysis.**
Joseph R. Harbert. PhD dissertation, City University of New York, 1984. 490p. bibliog.
Examines the impact of the general international system on those involved in internal conflict, and the social, political, economic and ideological environment in which they function. It also studies the influence of external political influences on events in Bolivia. Cuba, the Dominican Republic and Bolivia are used as case-studies.

224 **Los electorado sirven a la burguesía y al golpismo.** (The electorate serves both the middle class and military takeover.)
Guillermo Lora. La Paz: Masas, 1980. 67p.
An important pamphlet, which discusses the political crisis in Bolivia in the late 1970s, placing the blame on the liberal structure of the government and calling for radical change. A good example of political writing in the advocacy tradition.

225 **Fisonomía del regionalismo boliviano.** (Physiognomy of Bolivian regionalism.)
José Luis Roca.   La Paz: Editorial los Amigos del Libro, 1980. 419p. bibliog.

An excellent study of the continued importance of regionalism in Bolivian political and economic life. Regional rivalries are destructive to national development and are seen to be at the root of political problems.

226 **La guerra de insultos: la propaganda política en Bolivia, 1979.** (The war of insults: political propaganda in Bolivia, 1979.)
Raúl Rivadeneira Prada.   La Paz: Difusión, 1980. 259p. bibliog.

Examines political campaigning in Bolivia with a special emphasis on political advertising.

227 **The impact of revolution: a comparative analysis of Mexico and Bolivia.**
Susan Eckstein.   London; Beverly Hills, California: Sage Publications, 1976. 55p. bibliog. (Sage Professional Papers in Contemporary Political Sociology Series no. 06-016, vol. 2).

A comparative study of Latin America's two non-socialist revolutionary experiments.

228 **The military withdrawal from power in South America.**
Martin Needler.   *Armed Forces and Society*, vol. 6, no. 4 (1980), p. 614-24.

Traces the withdrawal from power of the Brazilian, Peruvian, Ecuadorian and Bolivian military establishments, and explains how and why the shifts in power occur. The role played by the United States in shaping events and decisions is also examined.

229 **Military's tight grip on South America: free elections in Peru are offset by a coup in Bolivia.**
*U.S. News* (18 Aug. 1980), p. 51-53.

The free-election/*golpe de estado* syndrome has been a part of Andean political culture since Independence.

230 **El mito de los partidos dominantes en la consolidación de revoluciones: una comparación entre México y Bolivia.** (The myth of the role of dominant parties in the consolidation of revolutions: a comparison between Mexico and Bolivia.)
*Revista Mexicana de Ciencia Política*, vol. 21, no. 80 (1975), p. 51-64.

Compares post-revolutionary developments in Mexico and Bolivia to demonstrate that the establishment of similar political institutions in dissimilar social environments does not produce the same results.

231 **Modern-day Bolivia: legacy of the revolution and prospects for the future.**
Edited by Jerry R. Ladman. Tempe, Arizona: Center for Latin American Studies, Arizona State University, 1982. 409p.
Presents scholarly essays prepared by experts for a conference on modern Bolivian issues. In addition to an historical overview, political development, the role of labour, the United States, the Sea issue, economic development and social change are also examined. Concludes that Bolivia's future is rather bleak.

232 **Political change, class conflict, and the decline of Latin American Fascism.**
James Petras. *Monthly Review*, vol. 31, no. 2 (1979), p. 26-37.
The development of protest against reactionary administrations has been observed in Latin America in the 1960s and 1970s. Here protest is studied in four different areas of Latin America, including Bolivia.

233 **The politics of antipolitics: the military in Latin America.**
Brian Loveman, Thomas Davies. Lincoln, Nebraska: University of Nebraska Press, 1978. 309p. bibliog.
This volume of forty-four articles, speeches and documents discusses Bolivian militarism in a comparative framework with Argentina, Brazil, Chile and Peru. It is primarily designed for classroom use and serves as a very competent introduction to a complex issue.

234 **Populism and political development in Latin America.**
A. E. van Niekerk. Rotterdam, The Netherlands: Rotterdam University Press, 1974. 230p. bibliog.
Deals with the problems of the functions of populism in Latin American political culture. The current practice of assessing populism as a political anomaly or a piece of regional folklore is unjust and misleading. A chapter entitled 'Populism and political agrarianism' deals with contemporary Bolivia.

235 **El populismo del MNR: divisiones y deformaciones.** (The populism of the MNR: divisions and distortions.)
Luis Antezana Ergueta. La Paz: [n.p.], 1983. 31p.
The actual title on the cover of this pamphlet is *Politics and the actual crisis.* Examines the current political crisis and how MNR policies contributed to its formation.

236 **Redemocratization in Latin America: the Andean pattern.**
James M. Malloy, Luis Abugatta. Hanover, New Hampshire: American Universities Field Staff, 1983. 10p. (South America Series, vol. 18).
Analyses the latest swing away from military rule to democracy in Peru, Ecuador and Bolivia.

237  **A reply to Lucien Goldmann.**
Herbert Marcuse.  *Partisan Review*, vol. 38, no. 4 (1971),
p. 397-400.

Marcuse and Goldmann hold differing theories on the role of students in Marxist revolutions. Here, Marcuse concludes that the student movement has played, and will continue to play, an important role in bringing about a true socialist-democratic system of world politics. His study includes Bolivian examples. See also Lucien Goldmann's 'Understanding Marcuse' (*Partisan Review*, vol. 38, no. 3 (1971), p. 246-62.).

238  **Revolution and the rebirth of inequality: a theory applied to the national revolution in Bolivia.**
Jonathan Kelley, Herbert S. Klein.  Berkeley, California:
University of California Press, 1982. 279p.

Examines the effects revolutions have on the people they liberated and argues that revolutions improve overall living standards, reduce inequality, and cause a decline in privilege. Education and skills are still not valued in Bolivian society, so revolution benefits those who are better off rather than the poorest members of society.

239  **The roads are not taken: institutionalization and political parties in Cuba and Bolivia.**
Jorge I. Domínguez, Christopher N. Mitchell.  *Comparative Politics*, vol. 9, no. 2 (Jan. 1977), p. 173-95.

Compares and contrasts the role of the political parties of Cuba and Bolivia in three important areas of the revolutionary process: mass political participation; the reorganization of society; and attitudes toward, and criticism of, the new régime.

240  **Socialism and Fascism in Latin America today.**
Theotonio Dos Santos.  *Insurgent Sociologist*, vol. 7, no. 4 (1977), p. 15-23.

Events in several Latin American nations, including Bolivia, suggest that the conflict between Fascism and socialism is not subsiding. The emergence of right-wing régimes and their opposition to an ever more radicalized working-class movement are seen as the initial steps in a movement towards permanent Fascism.

241  **Strategy for revolution.**
Regis Debray.  New York: Monthly Review, 1970, 255p.

A classic study of revolutionary tactics, strategy, and failure in Bolivia by a French Marxist who studied revolution in Third World countries, and accompanied Che Guevara to Bolivia, where Guevara's attempts to bring about revolution in 1964 failed, ending with his death.

242 **The urban character of contemporary revolutions.**
Josef Gugler. *Studies in Comparative International Development*,
vol. 17, no. 2 (1982), p. 60-73.

Compares the Cuban, Bolivian, Iranian, and Nicaraguan revolutions and
concludes that, contrary to the Skocpol thesis, based on the Chinese case-study,
successful revolutions are urban, not rural, in nature.

# Foreign Relations

## General

### 243 Latin American diplomatic history.
Harold E. Davis, John Finan, F. Taylor Peck. Baton Rouge, Louisiana: Louisiana State University Press, 1977. 301p. bibliog.

Emphasizes foreign relations among Latin American countries rather than their ties to external countries. For Bolivia this work deals with the War of the Santa Cruz Confederation (1836-39), the War of the Pacific (1879-84), the Chaco War (1932-35) and its numerous boundary problems with Peru and Brazil.

### 244 La relaciones internacionales en la historia de Bolivia.
(International relations in the history of Bolivia.)
Valentín Abecia Baldivieso. La Paz: Editorial los Amigos del Libro, 2 vols. (1979). bibliog.

The most recent and up-to-date survey of Bolivian foreign relations. Volume one traces events from pre-Columbian times, and the conquest of Caracas, to the 1874 treaty with Chile. Volume two concentrates on the War of the Pacific with Chile, and the Chaco War fought with Paraguay. Based on primary and secondary sources, this work provides a good introduction to foreign affairs.

# The Pacific Issue

**245 British policy in the War of the Pacific: Chile vs. Peru and Bolivia, 1879-1884. A chapter of free trade expansion in the pax britannica period (imperialism, periphery, bourgeoisie, indebtedness).**
Enrique Amayo-Zevallos. PhD dissertation, University of Pittsburgh, Pittsburgh, Pennsylvania, 1985. 373p. bibliog.

During the War of the Pacific, British and Chilean commitment to free trade transformed them into allies, against Peru, which desired to create a monopoly over nitrates. This 'alliance' was informal in nature.

**246 By reason or force: Chile and the balancing of power in South America, 1830-1905.**
Robert N. Burr. Berkeley, California: University of California Press, 1965. 322p. bibliog.

Awarded the Bolton Prize when published, this remains the best work in English on the subject of regional power struggles among South American nations. It analyses how Chile grew from a position of weakness to one of strength and authority in the international affairs of South America. Burr deals with the war of the Santa Cruz Confederation and the War of the Pacific.

**247 Casimiro Olañeta, diplomático, 1824-1839.** (Casimiro Olañeta, diplomat, 1824-39).
Blanca Gómez de Aranda. La Paz: Instituto Boliviano de Cultura, 1978. 121p. bibliog.

A biography of one of Bolivia's most important historical figures of the turbulent early years of Bolivia's national period. Like many 19th-century political figures, he had a variety of roles. In his role as a diplomat he guided Bolivia's fortunes admirably during the government of General Andrés de Santa Cruz in the 1830s.

**248 Chile, Perú y Bolivia independientes.** (Chile, Peru and independent Bolivia.)
Jorge Basadre. Barcelona, Spain; Buenos Aires: Salvat, 1948. 880p. maps. bibliog.

A brief, well-balanced survey of the origins and history of the War of the Pacific (1879-84) by Peru's most famous and important contemporary historian is included in this interpretative history of the southern Andean region.

**249 The Chilean-Bolivian Lauca River dispute and the OAS.**
R. D. Tomasek. *Journal of Interamerican Studies and World Affairs*, vol. 9, no. 3 (1967), p. 351-66. bibliog.

An examination of the ongoing dispute over the boundary between Chile and Bolivia, which was a result of the War of the Pacific. The specific issue examined here concerns water rights.

250 **Conflict in South America.**
R. N. Gwynne. *Geographical Magazine*, vol. 51 (1979), p. 398.
A brief examination of Chile's border problems with Argentina and Bolivia.

251 **En lugar del desastre: Bolivia y el conflicto peruano-chileno.** (In place of disaster: Bolivia and the Peruvian-Chilean conflict.)
Mariano Baptista Gumucio. La Paz: Editorial los Amigos del Libro, 1975. 105p. bibliog.
Discusses the border problems which developed between Peru, Bolivia and Chile as a result of the War of the Pacific.

252 **Guerra del Pacifico: analisis estrategico.** (War of the Pacific: strategic analysis.)
Victor Larenas Quijada. *Revue de Marina*, no. 3 (1982), p. 273-300; no. 5 (1982), p. 591-614; no. 1 (1983), p. 53-84.
Explores the possible causes of the War of the Pacific (1879-84) between Chile, Peru and Bolivia. Also includes details of the battles which took place.

253 **Hacia el mar: Bolivia's quest for a Pacific port.**
R. B. St. John. *Inter-American Economic Affairs*, vol. 31, no. 3 (1977), p. 27-73. bibliog.
Traces Bolivia's attempts to secure a suitable Pacific port since the era of Independence, through the War of the Pacific up to recent times. A useful survey of an extremely emotional and nationalistic issue.

254 **Historia gráfica de la Guerra del Pacífico.** (An illustrated history of the War of the Pacific.)
Mariano Baptista Gumucio. La Paz: Ultima Hora, 1978. 119p. 44 leaves.
A collection of photographs of Bolivian generals, soldiers, towns, ships, documents etc. relating to the War of the Pacific, 1879-84.

255 **A modern history of Peru.**
Frederick B. Pike. New York: Praeger, 1969. 386p. bibliog.
Discusses the Santa Cruz Confederation and the War of the Pacific, in chapters three, five and six, from the Peruvian point of view.

256 **The question of the Pacific: current perspectives on a long-standing dispute.**
Dennis R. Gordon. *World Affairs*, vol. 141, no. 4 (1979), p. 321-35. bibliog.
Describes the present status of the long-standing international dispute between Peru, Bolivia and Chile concerning the conflicting claims over the sea coast. The dispute is an outgrowth of the War of the Pacific (1879-84), during which Chile gained possession of the mineral-rich coastal regions of Peru and Bolivia.

# Border relations

257 **The Acre revolution, 1899-1903, a study of Brazilian expansion.**
Charles E. Stokes. PhD dissertation, Tulane University, New
Orleans, Louisiana, 1974. 483p. bibliog.
A scholarly study of the Acre issue in Bolivian–Brazilian relations. The province
of Acre was the site of the rubber boom at the beginning of this century.

258 **Bolivia-Brazil-Columbia-Ecuador-Guyana-Peru-Surinam-
Venezuela: treaty for Amazonian cooperation.**
*International Legal Materials*, vol. 11 (summer 1978), p. 1045-53.
A copy and discussion of the treaty which was signed on 3 July 1978 in Brasilia.

259 **Bolivian oil and Brazilian economic development.**
Peter S. Smith. *Journal of Interamerican Studies and World
Affairs*, vol. 13, no. 2 (1971), p. 274-77.
An examination of Brazilian attempts to corner the market of Bolivian oil
production.

260 **The boundary controversy in the upper Amazon between Brazil,
Bolivia and Peru, 1903-1909.**
F. Gunzert. *Hispanic American Historical Review*, vol. 14, no. 4
(1934), p. 427-49. bibliog.
An examination of the boundary dispute during the time of the rubber bonanza.
The discovery of rubber in Bolivia's Amazonian provinces created problems for
the national government because it was so remote from settled Bolivia, and
because the Bolivian government lacked effective control over the region. In the
competition for territory, Brazil was able to occupy and then seize the area.
See also J. V. Fifer's *Bolivia: land, location and politics since 1825* (q.v.).

261 **The Chiquitos affair: an aborted crisis in Brazilian–Bolivian
relations.**
Ronald L. Seckinger. *Luso-Brazilian Review*, vol. 11, no. 1
(1974), p. 19-40.
Discusses the potential conflict over Brazilian attempts to annex Chiquitos in
eastern Bolivia, in 1825. Fortunately, commonsense prevailed and war was
avoided.

262 **Foreign investment as an influence on foreign policy behavior: the
Andean Pact.**
Elizabeth G. Ferris. *Inter-American Economic Affairs*, vol. 33
no. 2 (1979), p. 45-69.
Examines government support of member nations for a policy of treating foreign
investment in a common manner. The Andean Common Market failed to

53

function because nations chose to place a greater priority on attracting foreign investment from the developed world than on acting in unison.

263 **National support for the Andean Pact.**
Elizabeth G. Ferris. *Journal of Developing Areas*, vol. 16, no. 2 (1982), p. 249-70.
An update on Bolivian participation in the Andean Pact.

264 **The politics of crisis and cooperation in the Andean group.**
William P. Avery. *Journal of Developing Areas*, vol. 17, no. 2 (1983), p. 155-84.
Progress toward regional co-operation has halted because of profound political and economic problems in the area. The instability of member governments and the fact that systems of government range from military dictatorships to democracies makes co-operation very difficult.

# With the United States

265 **The American legation in Bolivia, 1848-1879.**
Scott H. Shipe.    PhD dissertation, St. Louis University, St. Louis, Missouri, 1967. 568p. bibliog.
A study of 19th-century US relations with South America. The period covered begins after the Santa Cruz interlude and ends with the outbreak of the War of the Pacific.

266 **American oil companies in Latin America: the Bolivian experience.**
Herbert S. Klein. *Inter-American Economic Affairs*, vol. 18, no. 2 (1964), p. 47-72.
An examination of the state expropriation of American-owned companies in Bolivia and the reaction of the US government.

267 **Banzer's Bolivia.**
Laurence Whitehead. *Current History*, vol. 70, no. 413 (1976), p. 61-64.
Traces the efforts of the Hugo Banzer régime to negotiate with Chile on the matter of a Pacific seaport. Banzer was not very successful because he had too little to bargain with. Banzer's relations with the United States are also covered.

268 **The dismantling of the good neighbor policy.**
Bryce Wood. Austin, Texas: University of Texas Press, 1985.
290p. bibliog.
This volume is based on documents from the Public Records Office in London, the National Archive, and State Department data, and Wood provides here the conclusion to his classic study, *The making of the good neighbor policy*. The policy remained in effect during the Second World War, was codified in the Charter of the OAS in 1948, reasserted by President Truman in 1948-50, but then repudiated by Eisenhower in 1954. Includes a chronology which finishes in 1954.

269 **Economic aid and imperialism in Bolivia.**
Rebecca Scott. *Monthly Review*, vol. 24, no. 1 (1972), p. 48-60.
US economic aid to Bolivia during the period 1952-64 helped to transform the MNR movement from a radical popular front to an ally of the United States. The United States controlled and directed development strategies and US leverage can be seen in several areas: (1) the compensation paid to expropriated tin miners; (2) alteration of the Bolivian petroleum codes; (3) the establishment of an investment climate favourable to foreigners; and; (4) the unwillingness of the government of Bolivia to accept aid from socialist states.

270 **Fish, peasants and state bureaucracies: the development of Lake Titicaca.**
Román Laba. *Comparative Political Studies*, vol. 12, no. 3 (1979), p. 335-61.
Traces the attempts of the Peruvian, Bolivian and US governments to create a commercial fishing industry at Lake Titicaca and gives reasons explaining why the project failed.

271 **Foreign aid and revolutionary development: the case of Bolivia, 1952-1964.**
Bernard Wood. Ottawa, Canada: Carleton University, School of International Affairs, 1970. 40p.
Examines how US aid to Bolivia during the period from 1952 to 1964 influenced the actions of the MNR government.

272 **Good neighbor diplomacy: United States policies in Latin America, 1933-1945.**
Irwin F. Gellman. Baltimore, Maryland: Johns Hopkins University Press, 1979. 296p. bibliog.
Roosevelt's world-wide diplomacy was a set of actions and reactions to unique circumstances. Accidentally labelled the 'good neighbour' policy at the start of his first term, the phrase came to cover a complex totality of inter-American efforts from 1933 to 1945.

273 **The Hickenlooper Amendment as a determinant of the outcome of expropriation disputes.**
W. Kuhn.   *Social Science Journal*, vol. 15, no. 1 (1977), p. 71-81.
Notes that the Hickenlooper Amendment to the Foreign Assistance Act of the United States which was passed in 1962 does not increase respect for American property by host countries. This Amendment allows the US government to cut aid and cancel the sale of military equipment to nations which have confiscated US-owned property.

274 **The hovering giant: US responses to revolutionary change in Latin America.**
Cole Blasier.   Pittsburgh, Pennsylvania: University of Pittsburgh Press, 1979. 314p. bibliog.
Describes, compares and explains US response to revolutionary change in four Latin American states: Guatemala, Cuba, Mexico and Bolivia.

275 **In defense of neutral rights; the United States Navy and the wars of independence in Chile and Peru.**
Edward B. Billingley.   Chapel Hill, North Carolina: University of North Carolina Press, 1967. 266p. bibliog.
Examines the nature of US naval operations off the coasts of Chile and Peru during the Independence period. This activity is studied in the context of both the long-term and short-term impact on inter-American relations.

276 **Latin America, the U.S. and diplomacy: new books and old problems.**
Ryszard Stemplowski.   *Latin American Research Review*, vol. 15, no. 1 (1980), p. 206-10.
A review, by a Polish scholar, of recent trends in United States–Latin American diplomatic history. This study includes a review of F. Pike's, *The United States and the Andean republics: Peru, Bolivia and Ecuador* (q.v.).

277 **My missions for revolutionary Bolivia, 1944-1962.**
Víctor Andrade.   Pittsburgh, Pennsylvania: University of Pittsburgh Press, 1976. 200p. bibliog.
Víctor Andrade, Bolivian ambassador to the United States from 1944 to 1962, offers a unique perspective on United States–Bolivian relations. This work contains candid, and often awkward, views of United States' actions. Also includes descriptions of meetings with Franklin D. Roosevelt, Truman, and Eisenhower and accounts of how Andrade negotiated massive economic and military aid for Bolivia.

278 **The quiet experiment in American diplomacy: an interpretative essay on United States aid to the Bolivian revolution.**
G. Earl Sanders. *(The) Americas* (Academy of American Franciscan History), vol. 33, no. 1 (1976), p. 25-49.
Despite the US government's long distrust of the MNR, it did support the MNR régime when it came to power in 1952 and in the aftermath of the Castro victory in Cuba in 1959, the United States stepped up aid to the Bolivian state. This aid had a moderating effect on the MNR régime and strengthened the military sector as well. Thus, US leverage increased and the MNR remained in the American orbit of influence.

279 **South American journey.**
Frank Waldo. New York: Duell, Sloan & Pearce, 1943. 404p.
A marvellous example of the spirit of the good neighbour policy, and the cultural diplomacy of the Franklin D. Roosevelt presidency. During the Second World War, Nelson Rockefeller headed a special state department agency to foster better understanding among Americans. Frank Waldo was sent on a tour throughout South America and Bolivia was a stop *en route*.

280 **The United States and the Andean republics: Peru, Bolivia, and Ecuador.**
Frederick B. Pike. Cambridge, Massachusetts: Harvard University Press, 1977. 493p. maps. bibliog.
This book presents the reader with more than the title suggests. Pike provides a useful comparative study of the political and cultural development of the three republics and shows how Andean cultural patterns contrast sharply with those of the United States. From these contrasts in culture ensues a great deal of incompatibility between the two regions, and prospects for reducing this incompatibility are seen as slight.

281 **The United States and Bolivia; a case of neocolonialism.**
Laurence Whitehead. London: Haslemere Group Publications, 1969. 36p.
A study of US–Bolivian relations. Whitehead asserts that Europeans and Latin Americans see the United States as attempting to recolonize Latin America through the manipulation of aid and loans.

282 **The United States and the development of South America, 1945-1975.**
Samuel L. Baily. New York: Franklin Watts, 1976. 246p. bibliog. (New Viewpoints).
States that US policy, contrary to popular belief, has made it more, rather than less, difficult for Latin Americans to significantly reduce the level of poverty. The South American policy of the United States is not the result of a secret conspiracy among bankers and generals. Rather, it flows naturally from the pursuit of what US leaders believe to be in the national interest, coupled with ignorance and apathy on the part of the American population.

283 **The United States and Latin American wars 1932-1942.**
Bryce Wood.   New York: Columbia University Press, 1966. 519p.
bibliog.

Studies three modern wars in South America. Included here is a section (p. 19-137) on the Chaco War, the inter-American system and the peace process.

284 **U.S. coverage since 1952 of Bolivia: the unknown soldier of the Cold War.**
Jerry A. Knudson.   *Gazette (International Journal for Mass Communication Studies)*, vol. 23, no. 3·(1977), p. 185-97.

US radio services in their coverage of Bolivian politics perpetuated the view that Latin American nations can only function under military régimes. The author examines the cultural conditions which may have led reporters to make distorted assessments, and also states that Latin America is a low priority news area and, as a result of this low status, the area gets very poor news coverage. This lack of news enables the military establishment in the United States to have a stronger influence on foreign policy in the region.

285 **U.S. development assistance to rural Bolivia, 1941-1974: the search for development strategy.**
Lawrence C. Heilman.   PhD dissertation, American University, Washington, DC, 1982. 303p. bibliog.

Examines US government assistance to Bolivia to support rural development. The US strategy was the 'trickle-down' approach for developing agriculture in the Santa Cruz area.

# Cocaine traffic

286 **America on drugs.**
*U.S. News*, (28 July 1986), p. 48-55.

A general article on drug use in US society which also discusses the US military role in Bolivia's assault on the cocaine trade.

287 **Drugs and politics: an unhealthy mix.**
Michael Flatte, Alexei J. Cowett.   *Harvard International Review*, vol. 8 (1986), p. 29-31.

Discusses the relationships between the Bolivian government and the cocaine barons.

288 **Illicit drug traffic and U.S.–Latin American relations.**
Richard B. Craig. *Washington Quarterly*, vol. 8 (fall 1985)
p. 105-204.

Argues that the US government and general population is primarily interested in
Latin America because it is the major source of hard and soft drugs. The control
of drug cultivation, processing and shipping now ranks in importance in US eyes
with illegal immigration, the debt crises and fighting communism. Also looks at
US relations with Bolivia, Peru and Colombia.

289 **A laboratory approach to the control of cocaine in Bolivia.**
M. Moralesvaca. *Bulletin on Narcotics*, vol. 36, no. 2 (1984),
p. 33-43.

A discussion of how to manage the illegal drug traffic.

290 **Oversight on illegal drug trafficking from Bolivia and US**
**application of the Rangel Amendment.**
Washington, DC: US House of Representatives, Committee on
Banking, Finance and Urban Affairs, Subcommittee on International Development, Institutions and Finance, 1981. 15p.

Discusses whether the Rangel Amendment, which requires the United States to
vote against loans to nations which fail to take adequate measures to counter drug
trafficking, should be used against Bolivia. The Bolivian government was at this
time allegedly involved in the cocaine business.

291 **The role of the U.S. military in narcotics control overseas: hearing**
**before the Committee on Foreign Affairs, House of Representatives,**
**Ninety-ninth Congress, second session, August 5, 1986. (Role of the**
**U.S. military in narcotics control overseas).**
Washington, DC: US Government Printing Office, 1968. 65p.

Reviews the Reagan Administration's policy of using military personnel on drug
enforcement action overseas, and also examines Operation Blast Furnace in
Bolivia. The latter was not a US military operation but was executed and planned
by Bolivia.

292 **United States policies and strategies to control foreign production of**
**marijuana and cocaine: Peru, Bolivia, and Colombia.**
Carl P. Florez. *Police Studies*, vol. 8 (summer 1985), p. 84-92.
bibliog.

Discusses US policy options for improving its control over drug trafficking. The
United States depends on the DEA and the State Department to implement its
overseas policies.

# Constitution and Local Government

### 293 Constitution of Bolivia, 1967.
Washington, DC: Pan American Union (PAU), 1967. 41p.

This is a translation of the 1967 Constitution and forms part of the PAU series on laws and treaties.

### 294 Local government in Bolivia: public administration and popular participation.
Adrianne Aron-Schaar.   In: *Contemporary cultures and societies of Latin America; a reader in the social anthropology of Middle and South America.*   Edited by Dwight B. Heath. New York: Random House, 1974. 2nd ed. 572p. bibliog.

A case-study of graft in a small Bolivian town of 2,000 residents. The data focuses on how town officials supplement their low salaries and includes a taxonomy of graft. Despite the MNR revolution, local government remains hierarchical and corrupt.

# Statistics

295 **Boletín demográfico departamental: análisis de los resultados del censo nacional de población y vivienda de 1976.** (Departmental demographic bulletin: analysis of the results of the 1976 census.) La Paz: Instituto Nacional de Estadística. 3 vols.

The first three volumes of a projected nine-volume study of population trends in contemporary Bolivia. The results of the 1976 census are here reported for the departments of Chuquisaca, Cochabamba and Tarija.

296 **Bolivia: a commercial and industrial handbook.**
W. L. Schurz. Washington, DC: US Government Printing Office, 1921. 252p.

A survey of Bolivia's natural wealth, economic growth potential and trade possibilities, authorized by the Department of Commerce.

297 **Epidemological studies in Bolivia; final epidemological report of the Peace Corps.**
Abdel R. Omran. New York: Research Institute for the Study of Man, 1967. 260p.

Provides public health statistics for Bolivia gathered on a nation-wide basis. The study examines many types of communities, and focuses on tuberculosis, parasite infections and nutritional status. Omran's report is based on the idea that effective health promotion requires the technical knowledge of both the health and social sciences.

298  **República de Bolivia: proyecciones de población sexo y grupos de edad, años 1950 al 2000.** (Republic of Bolivia: projections of population by sex and age groups, years 1950 to 2000.)
Mario Gutiérrez S.   La Paz: Instituto Nacional de Estadística, Department de Estadísticas Sociales, División de Población y Vivienda, 1979. 56p.

This pamphlet on population trends in contemporary Bolivia is based on data from censuses and the United Nations.

# Environment

299 **Desastres naturales de 1982-1983 en Bolivia, Ecuador y Perú.** (The
natural disasters of 1982-83 in Bolivia, Ecuador, and Peru.)
Santiago, Chile: UN Economic and Social Council for Latin
America, 1984. 223p.

Discusses the natural disasters which have occurred recently in Bolivia, such as
drought in the highland areas and rain and flooding in the lowlands, caused by *El
Niño* (a spectacular oceanographic/meteorological phenomenon), which appears
at regular intervals, destroying food and agribusiness crops.

300 **Man in the Andes: a multidisciplinary study of high-altitude
Quechua.**
Edited by Paul Baker, Michael Little. Stroudsburg,
Pennsylvania: Dowden, Hutchinson & Ross, 1976. 482p. bibliog.

One of a series of volumes which report the research of US scientists participating
in the International Biological Programme. The purpose of the study is to gain a
better understanding of the structure and function of major ecological systems.
Topics reported on include: physical and biotic environment; child care; genetic
history; population movement and gene flow; fertility, morbidity and post-natal
mortality; pre-natal and infant growth; growth and morphology at high altitudes,
nutrition, pulmonary function and oxygen transport; haematology; work performance of newcomers; drug use; and physiological responses to cold.

301 **Water legislation in South American countries: Argentina, Bolivia,
Brazil, Chile, Colombia, Ecuador, French Guiana, Guyana,
Paraguay, Peru, Uruguay, and Venezuela.**
Mario Francisco Valls. Rome: Food and Agriculture Organization
of the UN, 1983. 171p.

A general survey of maritime and navigation legislation.

# Population

302  **A demographic and economic growth model for Bolivia.**
Anthony Picardi. *Simulation*, vol. 20, no. 4 (1973), p. 109-19.

Describes a two-sector population and economic stimulation model for Bolivia. Testing of the model indicates that average lifetimes and population growth rates vary considerably in response to both public health and family planning programmes, and growth-stimulating economic policies. Picardi suggests that birth-control incentive programmes should accompany those that are aimed at reducing the death rate.

303  **Evolutionary implications of the ethnography and demography of Ayoreo Indians.**
A. A. Pérez Diez, F. M. Salzano. *Journal of Human Evolution*, vol. 7, no. 3 (March 1978), p. 235-68. bibliog.

Presents demographic data for the unacculturated Ayoreo Indians of Bolivia. Also discusses fertility, mortality patterns and the implied evolutionary conclusions of their behaviour.

304  **Historia demográfica de las misiones de Mojos.** (Demographic history of the Mojos missions.)
Leandro Tormo. *Missionalia Hispanica*, vols 35-36 (1978-79), p. 285–309.

Study of the demographic aspect of the work of the Jesuits in Bolivia towards the end of the 17th century.

305  **The interrelationship of mortality and fertility in rural Bolivia.**
S. Stinson. *Human Biology*, vol. 54, no. 2 (1982), p. 299-313.

Examines death rates and correlates them with fertility figures taken from

64

Aymará populations in rural Bolivia. Demographic information was collected from 149 families of school-age children. Fertility and child mortality rates were similar to those of other highland villages, but the sex ratio at birth was lower than previously reported. Family size had no effect on child mortality. Large numbers of children are not considered to be a burden on a family.

306  **The La Paz census of 1970 with comments on other problems of counting people in a developing country.**
Richard W. Patch.  Hanover, New Hampshire: American Universities Field Staff, 1970. 12p. (West Coast South America Series, vol. 18, no. 12).

This census seriously under-counted population at a time when problems associated with over-population in La Paz were becoming acute. There are no reliable complementary statistics to aid in computing a correction factor.

307  **Population review 1970: Bolivia.**
Richard W. Patch.  Hanover, New Hampshire: American Universities Field Staff, 1972. 23p. (West Coast South America Series, vol. 17, no. 1).

Population maldistribution appears to be Bolivia's major problem. Enormous expenditure on the development of roads, communications and health services are necessary before colonization can match the natural population increase.

308  **Studies in Spanish American population history.**
Edited by David Robinson.  Boulder, Colorado: Westview Press, 1981. 274p.

Included in this collection of essays is a study by Brian Evans entitled *'Census enumeration in late seventeenth century Alto Perú: the numeración general of 1683-1684'* (p. 24-55).

# Minorities

## General

309 **Alemanes en Bolivia.** (Germans in Bolivia.)
Albert Crespo.    La Paz: Editorial los Amigos del Libro, 1978.
246p. bibliog.
A general introduction, complete with photographs, to Bolivia's German community, with an emphasis on the most prominent citizens.

310 **Andean ethnology in the 1970s: a retrospective.**
Frank Salomon.    *Latin American Research Review*, vol. 7, no. 2
(1982), p. 75-128. bibliog.
The 1970s witnessed an outpouring of research on Andean cultural themes which was sufficient to place Andean studies among the more well-established regional sub-specialities of anthropology. Among the historic factors which helped to produce this abundance was the emergence of a generation of field-workers trained by John Murra, John Rowe, Herman Trimborn and R. T. Zuidema. This essay points out the areas of progress in Andean ethnology since the 1970s and provides an excellent listing of materials. Serves both the specialist and the *aficionado*.

311 **The Bolivian Immigration Bill of 1942: a case study in Latin American anti-Semitism.**
Jerry Knudson.    *American Jewish Archives*, vol. 22, no. 2 (1970),
p. 138-58.
Investigates anti-Semitism prevalent in Bolivia during the Second World War, and attempts made by the Bolivian government to stop the immigration of Jews to Bolivia.

312 **Bolivian Indian tribes: classification, bibliography and map of present language distribution.**
Arnold Key, Mary Key. Norman, Oklahoma: University of Oklahoma Press, 1967. 124p.
Discusses what has been written about Bolivian Indian tribes and native languages of Bolivia. The text covers all native languages except Quechua and Aymará.

313 **The Chipaya of Bolivia: dermatoglyphis and ethnic relationships.**
Federico Murillo. *American Journal of Physical Anthropology*, vol. 46, no. 1 (1977), p. 45-50. bibliog.
Presents data on 15 dermatoglyphic traits collected from 141 Chipaya Indians. The biological relations were estimated through genetic distance measures involving biochemical poly-morphisms. Phylo-genetic relationships are compared with the linguistic and geographical distribution of this ethnic group.

314 **Handbook of South American Indians.**
Edited by Julian H. Steward. Washington, DC: US Government Printing Office, 1946-59. 7 vols.
The most important guide to present geographical, environmental, historical and cultural information concerning specific native peoples of South America.

315 **Historia del indigenismo cuzqueno, siglos XVI-XX.** (History of Cuzco nativism, 16th-20th centuries.)
Jose Tamayo Herrera. Lima: Instituto Nacional de Cultura, 1980. 394p.
This contribution to the expanding literature on peasant rebellions, written to commemorate the Túpac Amaru rebellion, provides a history of peasant awareness through the centuries of oppression.

316 **Los indios guarayos del Madre de Dios y del Beni.** (The Guarayo Indians of the Madre de Dios and Beni.)
Jehan Bellard. *Boletín del Instituto Riva-Aguero* (Peru), vol. 10 (1975-76), p. 139-67. bibliog.
Guarayo has been the name used since colonial times to refer to the groups of Indians living in the area of southeastern Peru and the Bolivian Chaco. Physiological and ethnological evidence has demonstrated that these two groups are related. These Indians, however, are not related to the Guaraní-speaking people of the Chaco region.

317 **Latin American Jewish studies.**
Judith Laiken Elkin. Cincinnati, Ohio: American Jewish Archives, 1980. 53p.
An inventory of the present status of studies pertaining to Latin American Jewry.

318 **Millenarianism as liminality: an interpretation of the Andean myth of Inkarri.**
   Mercedes López-Baralt. *Point of Contact*, vol. 2 no. 2 (1979), p. 65-80.

Examines and reproduces contemporary versions of the myths promising the return of the Incas. The myths are interpreted to reflect a return of the order and stability of the past, not an actual restoration of the historic empire.

319 **Native South Americans, ethnology of the least known continent.**
   Patrica Lyon. Boston, Massachusetts: Little, Brown, 1974. 433p. bibliog.

A first attempt to present in a single volume an introduction to the native cultures of South America. It includes essays by leading scholars. Good theoretical essays are included, together with articles based on field-work.

320 **Pueblos indígenas de Bolivia.** (Native people of Bolivia.)
   Dick Edgar Ibarra Grasso. La Paz: Librería y Editorial 'Juventud', 1985. 506p. maps. bibliog.

A comprehensive overview of Bolivia's complex indigenous culture which includes a discussion of: Quechua-speaking and Aymará-speaking Indians in the colonial era; the Urus and Chipayas of today; the Tacanas and Panos; the Lecos, Mosetenes and Yuracares; the Arawak nations of Bolivia; the Tupi-Guaraní in Bolivia; the Chiquitos, Bororos, Zamucos and Guatos; and the Tobas and Matacos of the far Chaco.

321 **Tawantinsuyu: cinco siglos de guerra gheswaymara contra España.**
   (Tawantinsuyu: five centures of native war with Spain.)
   Ankar, Chukiapu. La Paz: Centro de Coordinación y Promoción Campesina Minka, 1978. 557p.

An historical account of Indian–Spanish–Creole relations since the arrival of the Spaniards.

# Western Bolivia

322 **The Andean contrast.**
   Frank Salomon. *Journal of Interamerican Studies and World Affairs*, vol. 36, no. 1 (1982), p. 55-71.

Examines why the Quechua-speaking and Aymará-speaking Indians of Peru, Ecuador and Bolivia have been unable to mould themselves into effective political minorities. Compares Andean political culture, or lack of it, to the conditions in the Amazonian regions of the three respective countries.

323 **Andean societies.**
John V. Murra. *Annual Review of Anthropology*, vol. 13 (1984), p. 119-41. bibliog.
This is essential reading for anyone interested in the evolutionary development of the Andean region. It includes a scholarly review of ethnographic, ethnohistorical and historical trends in the region. Murra presents the state of research in a very readable, non-technical manner which is useful to both specialists and students alike.

324 **Awayqu Sumaj Calchapi: weaving, social organization, and identity in Calcha, Bolivia.**
Mary Ann Medlin. PhD dissertation, University of North Carolina at Chapel Hill, 1983. 338p. bibliog.
The Calcha, a Quechua-speaking Andean ethnic group in southern Potosí, weave cloth which the author argues is necessary for understanding their identity and social organization. The cloth recreates a shared identity and the Calcha weavers who are women, resist selling it because it explains their position in the world.

325 *Ayllu*: **el altiplano boliviano.** (*Ayllu*: the Bolivian highlands.)
Yolanda Bedregal, photographs by Peter McFarren. La Paz: Museo Nacional de Etnografía y Folklore, Editorial los Amigos del Libro, 1984. 94p.
Contains photographs, of varying quality, on traditional life cycles in highland villages.

326 **Los Aymará de Chichera, Perú: persistencia y cambio en un contexto bicultural.** (The Aymará of Chichera, Peru: persistence and change in a bicultural context.)
John Hickman. Mexico City: Instituto Indigenista Inter-americano, Sección de Investigaciones Antropolígicas, 1975. 221p. bibliog.
Another community study which examines the impact of mestizo culture on Aymará attitudes. Hickman concludes that these influences reinforce, rather than erode, Aymará culture.

327 **The Aymará of Chucuito, Peru. 1. Magic.**
Harry Tschopik. New York: American Museum of Natural History, 1951, p. 137-308. (Anthropological Papers of the American Museum of Natural History, vol. 44, part 2).
A study of the function of magic in an Aymará Indian community.

328 The Aymará of western Bolivia. Gene frequencies for eight blood
groups and nineteen protein and erythrocyte enzyme systems.
Robert Ferrell (et al.).   *American Journal of Human Genetics*,
vol. 30, no. 3 (1978), p. 539-49. bibliog.'
Electrophoresis was used to depict the level of poly-morphisms at 27 genetic loci
determining blood characteristics of 429 Aymará Indians. An extensive intra-
group genetic variation is presented, and rare biochemical variants are described.

329 The Aymará of western Bolivia: maxillofacial and dental arch
variation.
Hernán Palomino.   *American Journal of Physical Anthropology*,
vol. 49, no. 2 (1978), p. 157-66. bibliog.
Discusses the dimensions of the face, maxilla and dental arch present in the
Aymará population of Bolivia. Age, sex, and racial groups of the population are
noted.

330 The Aymará of western Bolivia: occluein, pathology and character-
istics of the dentition.
Hernán Palomino.   *Journal of Dental Research*, vol. 57, no. 3
(1978), p. 459-67.
A study of dental deformities and diseases among the Aymará Indians of Bolivia.
It offers comparisons with other Indian populations of Latin America.

331 Los Aymarás de las islas de Titicaca. (The Aymarás of the islands
of Lake Titicaca.)
Yaclav Solc.   Mexico City: Instituto Indigenista Interamericano,
1969. 194p. bibliog.
A study of the life-patterns among Aymará Indians of the Lake Titicaca islands.

332 The Bolivian Aymará.
Hans Buechler, Judith-Maria Buechler.   New York: Holt,
Rinehart & Winston, 1971. 114p. map. bibliog.
An excellent introduction to the Aymará peasant society of highland Bolivia for
the non-specialist, written by a team of respected anthropologists. It can also be
read as a community study of Compi, located near to Lake Titicaca, and describes
ritual and agricultural cycles.

333 Cabalgando entre dos mundos. (Between two worlds; the Aymará
of La Paz.)
Xavier Albó.   La Paz: CIPCA, 1983. 196p. bibliog.
Examines Aymará adjustment to urbanization by focusing on their experiences in
La Paz.

334 **Carnaval de Oruro; Tarabuco y Fiesta del Gran Poder.** (The Carnival of Oruro; Tarabuco and the Feast of the Great Power.) Augusto Beltrán Heredia (et al.). La Paz: Editorial los Amigos del Libro, 1977. 133p. bibliog.

Describes three of the principal folk festivals which occur annually in Bolivia. The traditional carnival celebrations occur on Fat Tuesday, the day before the beginning of Lent, and the Feast of the Great Power is celebrated in La Paz in late June, with all-day marching by members of special clubs wearing amazing costumes. A trip to Bolivia should be timed to view this absolutely magnificent day-long festival.

335 **Cultura aymará en La Paz: tradiciones y costumbres indígenas.** (The Aymará culture of La Paz: native traditions and customs.) Luisa Valda de Jaimes Freyre. La Paz: Imprenta y Librería Renovación, 1972. 199p.

An examination of Aymará folklore and folk culture. The author argues in favour of maintaining the continued vitality and significance of Aymará culture in the urban context.

336 **Ethnicity determination by names: a case study of validity and reliability in admixed groups in Chile and Bolivia.** R. Chakroborty, R. Ferrell, S. Barton. *American Journal of Physical Anthropology*, vol. 66, no. 2 (1985), p. 154.

The importance of surnames in genetic studies has been recognized for a century. In northern Chile and western Bolivia surname patterns enabled the classification of individuals on the basis of names into nine ethnic groups.

337 **Figura y carácter del indio (los andobolivianos).** (The face and character of the Bolivian Andean Indians.) Gustavo Otero. La Paz: Librería y Editorial 'Juventud', 1972. 203p.

A psycho-sociological examination of Bolivia's highland culture.

338 **Indians of the Andes: Aymarás and Quechuas.** Harold Osborne. Cambridge, Massachusetts: Harvard University Press, 1952. 266p. map. bibliog.

A classic study by an educated, non-specialist, observer and a good introduction to peasant societies. Its purpose is to trace the history and ecology of the Quechuas and the Aymarás from the scanty evidence which survives.

339 **The Kurahkuna of Yura: indigenous authorities in colonial Charcas and contemporary Bolivia.** Roger N. Rasnake. PhD dissertation, Cornell University, Ithaca, New York, 1982. 417p. bibliog.

Argues that the institution of the Kurahkuna, or indigenous authorities, is a key

71

factor in the Yuras' continuing ability to maintain cohesive social units and a cultural identity. The Yuras are a group of Quechua-speaking peasants in the Potosí area of Bolivia.

340 **The masked media: Aymará fiesta and social interaction on the Bolivian highlands.**
Hans Buechler. New York: Mouton, 1980. 399p. bibliog.

An examination of the rituals of the peoples of highland areas of Bolivia as instruments for transmitting information about ongoing social ties among the peoples involved. This information is only partly inherent in the symbolism of fiestas; the meanings are created during the performances. Buechler draws on a lifetime of research in the Andean highlands and concludes that the rituals generate, select, and present information about social ties.

341 **Mountain of the Condor: the metaphor and ritual in an Andean**
*ayllu*. Joseph W. Bastien. St. Paul, Minnesota: West Publishing Company, 1978. 227p. maps. bibliog.

A study of the rituals and beliefs of Aymará Indians associated with the sacred mountain of Kaata. Describes in detail the rituals associated with birth, hair-cutting, marriage and death. The study concludes that such shrines are 'metaphors of the ecological order'.

342 **Una odisea: buscar pega.** (An odyssey: looking for work.)
Xavier Albó. La Paz: CIPCA, 1982. 202p. bibliog.

Examines the problems Aymará peasants have in adjusting to urban life, with a special focus on securing employment in the La Paz area. A thoughtful, insightful study by a noted expert.

343 **Oprimados pero no vencidos: luchas del campesinado aymará y qhechwa de Bolivia, 1900-1930.** (Oppressed but not defeated: the struggle of the Aymará and Quechua peasants of Bolivia, 1900-1930).
Silvia Rivera Cusicanqui. La Paz: Historia Boliviana, 1984. 201p. bibliog.

A social and political history of Bolivian peasants' attempts to gain political, social and economic integration in the years before the Chaco War. An English version is available, entitled *Oppressed but not defeated. Peasant struggles among the Aymará and Qhechwa in Bolivia, 1900-1930* (Geneva: United Nations Research Institute for Social Development, 1987. 222p.).

344 **The plateau peoples of South America, an essay in ethnic psychology.**
Alexander A. Adams. London: G. Routledge & Sons, 1915. 134p. bibliog.

An excellent example of various racial theories which dominated man's thinking at the beginning of this century. By using the idea of 'progress', the book proves that the Aymará and Quechua Indians of South America are in the process of rapid social and cultural degeneration.

345 **Qollohuaya Andean body concepts: a topographical-hydraulic model of physiology.**
Joseph W. Bastien. *American Anthropologist*, vol. 87, no. 3 (1985), p. 595-611.
The Qollohuaya Andeans draw on lessons gained from their environments to understand and explain bodily functions and physiology.

346 **Qollahuaya rituals: an ethnographic account of the symbolic relations of man and land in an Andean village.**
Joseph W. Bastien. PhD dissertation, Cornell University, Ithaca, New York, 1973. 303p. bibliog.
An ethnological study of Qollahuayan rituals and their relationship to the geographical, social, temporal and legendary dimensions of Kaata, a canton in the department of La Paz.

347 **Rebeliones indígenas, quechua y aymarás: homenaje al bicentenario de la rebelión campesina de Túpac Amaru, 1780-1980.** (Quechua and Aymará native rebellions: homage to the two hundredth anniversary of the Túpac Amaru peasant rebellion, 1780-1980.)
Jorge Flores Ochoa. Cuzco, Bolivia: Centro de Estudios Andinos, 1980. 154p.
Examines the tradition of peasant rebellion against the Spanish colonizers and then against the government. Contrary to preconceived opinions, peasants are active defenders of their rights and land when they perceive threats to their stability. Also examines how, why, and when, rebellions are likely to occur.

348 **Señores e indios: acerca de la cultura quechua.** (Gentlemen and Indians: Quechuan culture.)
José María Arguedas. Montevideo, Uruguay: Arca, 1976. 259p.
An interpretative essay which explores native concepts of honour. The author was a leading Peruvian poet and novelist who wrote in the Quechua language and from an Indian viewpoint.

349 **State, *ayllu* and ethnicity in northern Potosí, Bolivia.**
R. A. Godoy. *Anthropos*, vol. 80, nos 1-3 (1985), p. 53-65.
Discusses how Andean ethnic groups interact with one another, and focuses on the Jukumanis of northern Potosí.

350 **The technology of self-respect: cultural projects among Aymará and Quechua Indians.**
Patrick Breslin. *Grassroots Development*, vol. 6, no. 1 (1982), p. 33-37.
Describes two projects in Bolivia. The first is among Aymará Indians in the highlands and is an attempt to save, record and reanimate Aymará folk tales for the rural radio network. The other is located in Sucre and is concerned with reintroducing Quechua musical dance forms.

351 **Those who divide us: resistance and change among pastoral *ayllus* in Ulla Ulla, Bolivia.**
Deborah A. Caro. PhD dissertation, Johns Hopkins University, Baltimore, Maryland, 1985. 371p. bibliog.
Examines relations between alpaca herding communities, the wool market and the state in the Ulla Ulla area of Bolivia.

352 **Tribes of the Montana and Bolivian east Andes.**
Julian H. Steward. In: *Handbook of South American Indians.*
Edited by Julian H. Steward. Washington, DC: US Government Printing Office, 1948, vol.3, p. 507-657. bibliog.
A basic guide to highland cultures which indicates the problems involved in trying to summarise ethnological observations made over several centuries.

# Eastern Bolivia

353 **The aboriginal cultural geography of the Llanos of Mojos, a seasonally inundated savanna in northeastern Bolivia.**
William Denevan. Berkeley, California: University of California Press, 1966. 185p. maps. bibliog.
This volume is regarded by many as an excellent example of cultural geography. It demonstrates the need for archaeological studies to determine the sequential use of the land. Based on the field-observations of a professional geographer, the subjects covered include Savanna tribes, village patterns, and agriculture and demographic trends.

354 **The Ayoréode-Zapacó communal sawmill: a social forestry project in eastern Bolivia.**
Shelton H. Davis. *Grassroots Development*, vol. 9, no. 2 (1985), p. 2-9.
Discusses the socio-economic impact of a sawmill on this specific, traditional community. The Ayoréode accepted the sawmill because of its favourable social,

economic and cultural impact, specifically on employment, incomes and improved housing. The isolation of the village was also reduced.

355 **An evolutionary ecological analysis of the social organization of the Ayoreo of the northern Gran Chaco.**
Paul Emery Bugos. PhD dissertation, Northwestern University, Evanston, Illinois, 1986. 351p. bibliog.

Describes and explains the social organization of the Ayoreo people of south-eastern Bolivia and northern Paraguay. Included are discussions of the Ayoreo's physical and social environments, their economy, political system, kinship terminology and marriage practices, and their life cycle, descent, acculturation and residence.

356 **The native tribes of eastern Bolivia and western Matto Grosso.**
Alfred Métraux. Washington, DC: US Government Printing Office, 1984. 180p. map. (Smithsonian Institution, Bureau of American Ethnology, Bulletin 134).

Eastern Bolivia is an 'el dorado' for anthropologists because the region is peculiar in possessing an unusually large number of linguistic groups: Tupi-Guaraní, Arawaken, Cariban, Tacanu, Panoan, Chapakuran, Itonaman, Chiquitoan and Otarean. Provides a basic source of information on these Indian cultures.

357 **The native tribes of Mato Grosso and eastern Bolivia.**
Alfred Métraux. Washington, DC: US Government Printing Office, 1942. 182p. map. bibliog.

Discusses the following tribes: the Paressi, Chuquitos, Mojo and Baure. Also covers the Canichana, Movima, Cayavava, Itonama, Guarayu, Pauserna, Tacanan, Chirquano, Chane and the Leco.

358 **No longer nomads: the Sirionó revisited.**
Allyn MacLean Stearman. Lanham, Maryland: Hamilton Press, 1987. 166p. bibliog.

A new study of the Sirionó Indians.

359 **Peaceful societies: an introduction.**
David Fabbro. *Journal of Peace Research*, vol. 15, no. 1 (1978), p. 67-83.

Examines the social preconditions of the peaceful environment of the Sirionó people of eastern Bolivia. Peaceful communities tend to have similar character-istics. They are small, face-to-face communities with egalitarian social structures. They lack formal patterns of rank and stratification and place few, or no, restrictions upon the number of people who can exercise authority, or occupy positions of importance and prestige.

360 **The Sirionó of eastern Bolivia: a reexamination.**
Barry Issac. *Human Ecology*, vol. 5, no. 2 (1977), p. 137-54.
A study of the deculturation process among the Sirionó Indians of Bolivia.

361 **A study of the Sirionó Indians.**
Stig Ryden. Gothenburg: Humanistic Foundation of Sweden, 1941. 167p. map. bibliog.
An ethnological survey of the Sirionó Indians of eastern Bolivia. The material culture of the Sirionó is described as meagre and the tribe can be classified as one of the most primitive in the world. They were found to lack 'spiritual culture.'

362 **Unusual blood genetic characteristics among the Ayoreo Indians of Bolivia and Paraguay.**
Francisco Solano (et al.). *Human Biology*, vol. 50, no. 2 (1978), p. 121-36. bibliog.
Thirty-three serological and one salivary protein poly-morphisms were examined in 363 Ayoreo Indians from three localities. The populations were unacculturated and intra-tribally exogamous.

363 **The Yugui connection: another look at Sirionó deculturation.**
Allyn MacLean Stearman. Orlando, Florida: *American Anthropologist*, vol. 86, no. 3 (Sept. 1984), p. 630-50.
Demonstrates that the Yugui and Sirionó share the same cultural heritage and that the Sirionó are now acculturated while the Yugui are still in the process of acculturation. Thus, the Yugui offers a current example from which new insights into the Sirionó can be gained.

# Employment and Trade Unions

## General

364  **Los braceros bolivianos; drama humano y sangría nacional.** (The
Bolivian wetbacks; human and bloody national drama.)
Fernando Antezana.   La Paz: Editorial 'Icthus', 1966. 44p. map.
Chronicles the activities of the Bolivian migrant worker, who is forced to work in
neighbouring countries for low wages because of a lack of employment
opportunities at home. The migrant issue is considered to be a national disgrace.

365  **Economic transformation of Bolivia.**
Carter Goodrich.   Ithaca, New York: Cornell University Press,
1955. 38p.
A newsman's account of the exploitative labour system which existed in Bolivia
prior to 1952. A readable and useful introduction to pre-1952 labour conditions.

366  **Labor exploitation on pre-1952 haciendas in the lower valley of
Cochabamba, Bolivia.**
Stephan M. Smith.   *Journal of Developing Areas*, vol. 11, no. 2
(1977), p. 227-44.
An historical account of the regular exploitation of peasant labour in the rich
Cochabamba valley. This area during the 1952 revolution was the heart of peasant
militancy. The posture adopted by the peasants stemmed from their chronic
mistreatment.

367 **Measuring rural underemployment in Bolivia: a critical review.**
Clarence Zuvekas, Jr. *Inter-American Economic Affairs*, vol. 32
(spring 1979), p. 65-83.
Outlines the problems which confront researchers when attempting to calculate
the levels of underemployment and unemployment in a country such as Bolivia.

368 **Migration, ethnicity and adaptation: Bolivian migrant workers in
northeast Argentina.**
Scott Whiteford, Richard Adams. In: *Migration and urbanization: models and adaptive strategies.* Edited by Brian M. Du Toit
and Helen I. Safa. The Hague, Paris: Mouton, 1975, p. 179-99.
bibliog.
Adams uses Whiteford's data to study Bolivians who migrate to Argentina to
work in the sugar harvest. He develops typologies of peasants and examines
migratory stages.

369 **The participation of women in economic activity in Argentina,
Bolivia and Paraguay.**
Catalina H. Wainerman. *Latin American Research Review*,
vol. 15, no. 2 (1980), p. 143-51.
A short introduction to the role of women in economic development. The author
concludes that women in Bolivia find employment mainly in industries with low-
levels of technological innovation, and in agriculture. Lack of education is an
obstacle to women's employment in other areas; the exceptions are those women
who belong to the upper and middle classes.

370 **Unemployment and underemployment in Bolivian agriculture: a
critical survey of the literature.**
Washington, DC: US Department of Agriculture, International
Division; Bureau for Latin America, Rural Development Division,
1977. 70p. bibliog.
A critical review of rural unemployment, internal and external migration, wage
rates and governmental involvement in rural Bolivian life.

371 **Workers from the north: plantations, Bolivian labor and the city in
northwest Argentina.**
Scott Whiteford. Austin, Texas: University of Texas Press, 1981.
189p. map. bibliog.
Studies the relationships between land, labour and the city in the frontier area of
north-west Argentina. Bolivian agricultural workers are annually forced to leave
Bolivia and seek employment in neighbouring Argentina.

# Trade unions

**372 The Andean rural proletarians.**
Thomas Greaves. In: *Ideology and social change in Latin America*. Edited by June Nash, Juan Corradi, Hobard Spalding, Jr. New York: Gordon & Breach, 1977. 305p. bibliog.
Discusses the role of peasant syndicates in contemporary Bolivian political and economic life.

**373 Autonomy overshadowed: a Bolivian cooperative within the nationalized mining industry.**
Doris W. Widerkehr. *Human Organization*, vol. 30, no. 2 (1980), p. 153-60.
A study of a Bolivian mining community, organized as a workers' co-operative during the 1970s, and owned by the state corporation, COMIBOL. This institution tends to dominate local history.

**374 Historia de los sindicatos campesinos: un proceso de integración nacional en Bolivia.** (A history of peasant unions: a process of national integration in Bolivia.)
Luis Antezana E. La Paz: Consejo Nacional de Reforma Agraria, 1973. 436p.
This interesting and sympathetic study traces the history of peasant unions from the creation of the first syndicates in Cliza and Vacas in 1936, and considers their struggle against the socio-economic and political power structures. The second part deals with the era of passive resistance, from 1940 to 1946, and the post-1947 era. This was a period of reinvigorated struggle which led to the MNR triumph in April 1952 and the passage, and implementation, of the Agrarian Reform Bill in 1953. The account finishes in 1956.

**375 A history of the Bolivian labour movement, 1848-1971.**
Guillermo Lora. London: Cambridge University Press, 1977. 408p. bibliog.
An abridged and translated edition of Lora's five-volume history of the Bolivian labour movement. Trade unionism in Bolivia played a fundamental role in bringing about the MNR revolution of 1952. This is an excellent account of major political events and ideological issues which gave the Bolivian labour movement a splendid and complex history. This is the best single volume on this subject.

**376 Labor unions and political socialization: a case study of Bolivian workers.**
John H. Magill. New York: Praeger, 1974. 291p. map. bibliog.
Many workers in developing areas of the world are subjected to a process of political learning merely by belonging to a trade union. Through the official

activities of the union, the members are involved in a constant interaction with the political system. This is a study of the role of four Bolivian trade unions as agents of political change. The groups – miners, factory workers, peasants and petroleum workers – represent a variety of socio-economic and political backgrounds. This study deals with nation-building and the mass mobilization of citizens.

377  **La lucha del pueblo boliviana.** (The struggle of the Bolivian people.)
Fernando Arauco. *Revista Mexicana de Ciencias Politicas y Sociales*, vol. 21, no. 82 (1975), p. 57-70.

Examines Bolivian opposition to the US-imposed Banzer dictatorship of the 1970s. This opposition was orchestrated by two powerful syndicates: the Federation of Bolivian Mine Workers and the Bolivian Workers Central Organization.

378  **El movimiento obrero boliviana, 1935-1943.** (The Bolivian labour movement, 1935-43.)
Luis Antezana E.  La Paz: Editorial los Amigos del Libro, 1961. 71p.

A brief introduction to the history of the labour movement in Bolivia in the aftermath of the Chaco War. The labour movement was critical to the development of the MNR, and the author provides an introduction to its evolution in his narrative of the pre-1945 period.

379  **Política laboral en el Grupo Andino.** (Labour policy in the Andean Group.)
Luís Aparicio Valdez.  Lima: Universidad del Pacífico, 1972. 262p. bibliog.

An analysis of the current situation existing in the Andean Pact and attempts made to harmonize legislation concerning labour relations.

380  **La revolución campesina en Bolivia: historia del sindicalismo campesino.** (Peasant revolution in Bolivia: a history of peasant syndicalism.)
Luis Antezana E.  La Paz: Editorial 'Siglo', 1983. 112p.

This condensed version of the author's *Historia de los sindicatos campesinos: un proceso de integración nacional en Bolivia* (q.v.) provides a readable interpretative study of the evolution of peasant activism. Documents and various declarations are included in the appendixes.

381 **The strategy of peasant mobilization, some cases from Latin America and southeast Asia.**
Huizer Gerrit. *Development from below, anthropologists and development situations*. The Hague: Mouton, 1976, p. 221-54 bibliog.

Examines the role of peasant syndicates in Cochabamba, Bolivia. The peasants of the Cochabamba area have been involved in political activity since the 1940s.

382 **Worker consciousness and union organization: the problem of ideology and practice in Bolivian tin mines.**
June Nash. *Ideology and social change in Latin America*. Edited by June Nash, Juan Corradi, Hobard Spalding, Jr. New York: Gordon & Breach, 1977, p. 113-41. bibliog.

Studies miners' attitudes in order to gain a better understanding of how they can best be utilized in national politics.

383 **Workers' participation in the nationalized mines of Bolivia.**
June Nash. In: *Peasants, primitives and proletariats*. Edited by David Browman, Ronald Schwartz. New York: Mouton, 1979, p. 311-27.

Traces the struggles concerning worker participation in the Bolivian mining industry through a discussion of the organizational problems related to worker mobilization. Worker participation in Bolivia has failed to introduce substantial changes in working conditions; neither has it led to the miners playing a greater role in mine management.

384 **Workers' participation in the management of the Bolivian Mining Corporation.**
Manuel Olave. *Public Enterprise*, vol. 6 (May 1986), p. 239-45.

Discusses labour-management relations in Bolivia's national mining corporation. A highly favourable review of the efforts of the Bolivian Mining Corporation (COMIBOL) to make workers' participation function.

# Economy

## General

385 **The bankers in Bolivia, a study in American foreign investment.**
Margaret Alexander Marsh.   New York: Vanguard Press, 1928.
233p.
A now classic study of the penetration of foreign economic influence into an underdeveloped economy.

386 **Bolivia, its people and its resources, its railways, mines, and rubber forests.**
Paul Walle, translated by Bernard Maill.   London: T. F. Unwin, 1914. 407p.
An extensive description of Bolivia's potential wealth in the early 20th century, by a British minister of commerce. He praises the hardiness and excellent work habits of the 'popular classes' and believes that this mestizo race will guarantee Bolivia an economic bonanza in the future.

387 **Bolivia: nacion en desarrollo.** (Bolivia: a nation in development.)
José Romero Loza.   La Paz: Editorial los Amigos del Libro, 1974. 457p. bibliog.
Discusses the questions surrounding economic development in South America, and reviews the issues, and reasons for, and against, economic union and co-operation between natural trading partners.

388 **Bolivia: needs and prospects.**
New York: First National City Bank, 1965. 11p.
A short summary of the main features of the Bolivian economy of the mid-1960s.

389 **Bolivia: país saqueado.** (Bolivia: a ravaged country.)
Wagner Terrazas Urquidi. La Paz: Camarlinghi [n.d.]. 183p.
bibliog.
Discusses the natural resources of Bolivia and the progress of the conservation
effort. Calls for a more pragmatic economic policy.

390 **La economía de Bolivia.** (The economy of Bolivia.)
Eduardo Arze Cuadros. La Paz: Editorial los Amigos del Libro,
1979. 578p. maps.
A survey of Bolivian economic history from 1492 to 1979, translated from French
(originally a dissertation from the University of Paris). Included are theoretical
chapters dealing with: dependency theory; regionalism; the historical context of
regional development; the development of regional economic inequality; and the
organization of regional development. The conclusions address the issue of
regionalism and national integration. This represents a very competent work and
an excellent starting place for students, scholars and interested general readers
alike.

391 **The economic networks of Bolivian political brokers: revolutionary
road to fame and fortune.**
Madeline Barbara Leóns. *Peasant livelihood: studies in economic
anthropology and cultural ecology.* Edited by Rhoda Halperin,
Dow Halperin. New York: St Martin's Press, 1977, p. 102-16.
A case-study of economic and political life in the Bolivian Yungas which
concentrates on a man who has a large local clientele of debtors who repay their
loans with cash, crops, or favours.

392 **How economically consequential are revolutions? A comparison of
Mexico and Bolivia.**
Susan Eckstein. *Studies in Comparative International Development,* vol. 10, no. 3 (1975), p. 48-62.
Social revolutions in Bolivia and Mexico produced varying consequences. Bolivia
received more US support than any other Latin American country from 1952 to
1964, but did not generate a domestic capitalist class. In Mexico, a productive
industrial/agricultural economy has appeared. The two case-studies indicate that
economic growth depends upon how the state uses its power.

393 **Inflation and development in Latin America; a case history of
inflation and stabilization in Bolivia.**
George Jackson Eder. Ann Arbor, Michigan: Program in
International Business, Graduate School of Business
Administration, 1968. 822p. bibliog.
The author headed an economic mission in Bolivia (1956-57) to advise on
stabilization measures. He provides readers with a detailed description of the
obstacles which prevent inflation from being controlled.

394 **Informativo económico de Bolivia.** (Economic information for Bolivia.)
René González.   La Paz: Editorial los Amigos del Libro, 1974.
162p.
A short review of the economic conditions which existed in Bolivia in the 1970s.

395 **The post-war Latin American economies: the end of the long boom.**
Julio G. López.   *Banca Nazionale del Lavoro, Quarterly Review*,
(summer 1985), p. 233-60. bibliog.
Discusses the decline of Latin American growth in an historical context. The long-range perspective offers a new positive interpretation to what is generally gloomy reading.

396 **The stablization programs of the International Monetary Fund: the case of Bolivia.**
Melvin Burke.   *Marxist Perspectives*, vol. 2, no. 2 (1979),
p. 118-33.
The International Monetary Fund (IMF) induced the Bolivian government to retreat from the gains of the social revolution of 1952 in order to ensure price stability.

# Andean Pact

397 **The Andean Group at the ten year mark.**
Gordon Mace.   *International Perspectives* (Ottawa), Sept.–Dec.
1979, p. 30-34.
The Cartagena Agreement of 1969 initiated the process of economic integration among Andean Pact members. The encouraging progress of the first four years ended in 1974 primarily because of changes in the economic development models of member nations and also because of the loss of Chile as a Pact member. The Pact has been unable to avoid the difficulties that have affected similar efforts in the Third World.

398 **Foreign investment as an influence on foreign policy behavior.**
Elizabeth Ferris.   *Inter-American Economic Affairs*, vol. 33, no. 2
(1979), p. 45-69.
Shows how the six governments which constitute the Andean Pact act in support of the Pact and examines their decision to adopt a common approach towards foreign investment.

399 **Grupo andino y golpe de estado.** (Andean Pact and military takeover.)
Remo di Natale. La Paz: Letras, 1980. 101p. bibliog.
Discusses the Andean Common Market and the effect chronic political instability and continuous military takeovers have had upon economic development and trade.

400 **Le Pact andin: un processus positif d'intégration en Amérique latine.** (The Andean Pact: a positive process of integration in Latin America.)
Marcos Alvarez García. *Revue de l'Institute de Sociologie* 3-4, (1975), p. 415-36.
Discusses the Pact's objectives, achievements and future prospects. The Pact was an attempt to bring about the economic integration of Bolivia, Chile, Ecuador, Peru and Venezuela.

401 **Whither the Andean Pact?**
Thomas G. Sanders. Indianapolis, Indiana: *UFSI Reports*, (1985), 10p.
The post-1980 recession has posed the greatest challenge yet to the Pact's survival, though new initiatives, such as those presented by the Andean Business Consultation Council, hold some promise for the future.

# Development

402 **Bolivia: agricultural pricing and investment policies.**
Washington, DC: World Bank, 1984. 130p. bibliog.
Examines the economic aspects of agriculture, agricultural prices, government agricultural policy and the World Reconstruction and Development Bank's role in modernizing Bolivia's agricultural sector.

403 **The Bolivian economy, 1952-65; the revolution and its aftermath.**
Cornelius M. Zondag. New York: Praeger, 1966. 262p. bibliog.
An introduction to Bolivian contemporary society and the forces which shaped it prior to 1952. Included here is an analysis of the impact of the 1952-53 reforms on the national economy and on society. Zondag viewed economic development in a long-term perspective and concluded with the prediction that Bolivia had a promising economic future.

**Economy.** Development

404 **Integrated regional-development planning – linking urban centers and rural-areas in Bolivia.**
Da Rondinelli, H. Evans. *World Development* (New York), vol. 11, no. 1 (1983), p. 31-53.
Examines the potential for developing meaningful regional planning in Bolivia.

405 **The limits of industrialization in the less developed world: Bolivia.**
Susan Eckstein, Frances Hagopian. *Economic Development and Cultural Change*, vol. 32, no. 1 (1983), p. 63-95.
Asserts that Bolivia has been unable to industrialize because of prejudice amongst investors, the vested interests of local élites and general political constraints.

406 **Transformation of a revolution from below, Bolivia and international capital.**
Susan Eckstein. Boston, Massachusetts: *Comparative Studies in Society and History*, vol. 25, no. 1 (1983), p. 105-35.
Argues that, in the 1960s, foreign capital became so important to development that it contributed to the breakdown of the populist coalition which brought the MNR to power. In particular, capital benefited large-scale farmers who in the 1940s became a political force of some consequence. See also Susan Eckstein's 'Revolutions and the restructuring of national economies: the Latin American experience' (*Comparative Politics*, vol. 17 (July 1985), p. 473-94).

# Banking and Finance

407 **Bolivia moratorium – one answer to the debt crisis.**
C. Wise. *Nation*, vol. 239, no. 15 (1984), p. 476-78.
A brief discussion of attempts to combat Bolivia's severe economic and financial problems.

408 **Bolivia's economic crisis.**
James M. Malloy. *Current History*, vol. 86, no. 516 (Jan. 1987), p. 9-12.
A short informative review of Bolivia's present economic and financial crisis and the government's attempts to check inflation and foster growth.

409 **External debt in Bolivia.**
Robert Devlin, Michael Mortimore, United Nations Economic Commission for Latin America and the Caribbean. Boulder, Colorado: Westview Press, (forthcoming, 1988). approx. 300p.

410 **Hyperinflation: taming the beast.**
*Economist* (London), vol. 301 (15 Nov. 1986), p. 55-56.
Since 1985 four countries with very high rates of inflation have adopted controversial cures with mixed results. Bolivia's anti-inflation programme is the most remarkable. Victor Paz Estenssoro, after assuming office, removed controls on prices, interest rates, exports and imports; he legalized the black market and let the pesos reach its market value. It crashed to seven per cent of its previous value against the dollar and within one month the rate of inflation was one thousand per cent. It has now settled down to about fifty per cent annually. Also discusses inflation in Brazil, Argentina and Israel.

**Banking and Finance**

411   **International commercial bank lending to Third World countries, 1970-1981. An analysis of U.S. bank behavior.**
Claudia Helene Dziobek.   PhD dissertation, University of Massachusetts, Amherst, 1984. 202p. bibliog.
Examines the nature of, and rationale for, private US bank lending to Third World nations in the 1970s. Analyses twelve major banks and three countries: Jamaica, Peru and Bolivia. It is suggested that the banks were not concerned with how finance would be used, but were more interested in a country's political creditworthiness.

412   **Latin American hyperinflations.**
John Heyde (et al.). *Harvard International Review*, vol. 9 (March 1987), 36p.
A short review of Bolivia's galloping inflation.

413   **Memoria Anual Gestión 1980.** (Annual Report 1980.)
Banco Central de Bolivia.   La Paz: Banco Central de Bolivia, 1981. 174p.

414   **Power and the IMF (International Monetary Fund): the example of Bolivia.**
*Euromoney* (London), (Jan. 1982), p. 104.
Discusses the international political importance of the IMF. Because of its faith in its power, it acts but never inspires nations to rebuild their economies.

415   **Surgery without anaesthesia: Bolivia's response to economic chaos.**
Jennifer L. Bailey, Knutsen L. Torbjorn.   *World Today* (London), vol. 43 (March 1987), p. 47-51.
A readable, popular and informative survey of Bolivia's economic problems.

# Agriculture

## General

416 **Agricultural cooperatives: perspectives from the Aymará and the Bolivian state.**
Carlos Augusto Pérez-Crespo. PhD dissertation, State University of New York at Binghamton, New York, 1986. 293p. bibliog.
Examines changes in an Aymará community since 1953 in order to understand why peasants continue to organize agricultural co-operatives when these ventures are not successful. Among Algamani farmers the co-operative plays a political role in defending peasant rights.

417 **An analysis of the variables that affect the economic behavior of farm households in the southern valleys area of Bolivia.**
Lloyd C. Brown, Hydle Van de Wetering. La Paz: Ministerio de Asuntos Campesinos y Agropecuarios; United States Agency for International Development, 1982. 210p.
Examines how and why farmers allocate their economic resources as they do.

418 **El capitalismo mundial y la revolución agraria en Bolivia.** (World capitalism and agricultural revolution in Bolivia.)
Susan Eckstein. *Revista Mexicana de Sociología*, vol. 41, no. 2 (1979), p. 457-78. bibliog.
Thorough and comprehensive agricultural reform is difficult to achieve in contemporary Latin America because of the constraints imposed by international capitalistic structures.

419 **Commercial agriculture and peasant production: a case study of agrarian reformism and the development of capitalism in northern Santa Cruz, Bolivia (Latin America).**
Lesley J. Gill. PhD dissertation, Columbia University, New York, 1984. 306p. bibliog.

Examines the impact of cash crop development and foreign aid on the socio-economic position of peasant settlers in the frontier regions of Santa Cruz. The principal argument is that capitalism led to greater social differentiation and transformed a large strata of the peasants into a modern labour force.

420 **Common-property rangeland and induced neighborhood effects: resource misallocation in Bolivian agriculture.**
La Paz: Consortium for International Development (CID), 1976. 35p.

Measures must be taken immediately to prevent the destruction of arable lands in traditional agricultural areas. This work offers a variety of measures based on economic models, designed to decrease erosion by half.

421 **Economic and political implications of a rural Bolivian cooperative.**
W. Leóns. *International Social Science Review*, vol. 57, no. 4 (1982), p. 226-31.

Examines how an agricultural co-operative provides peasants with an opportunity to acquire political awareness and skills.

422 **Effects of a customs union on the nitrogenous fertilizer industry in the Andean zone.**
Carlos Banante, Richard Simmons. *Journal of Common Market Studies*, vol. 14, no. 3 (1976), p. 255-75.

Discusses agricultural technology and development within the context of regional problems.

423 **An elusive harvest: the process of a Bolivian cooperative movement.**
Wendy R. Demegret. PhD dissertation, New York University, New York, 1984. 397p. bibliog.

Examines a multi-service co-operative movement in Chuquisaca, an under-developed agricultural region. It explores how and why co-operatives are promoted as instruments of social change and development and how they are affected by the environment.

424 **The emergence of agricultural forms of production in the Santa Cruz region of eastern Bolivia.**
James Kirkpatrick Patton. PhD dissertation, Washington University, St. Louis, Missouri, 1983. 258p. bibliog.

Since the agrarian reform of 1953, two forms of agriculture have emerged in Santa

Cruz: large, capitalist farms which produce for the national and international market; and a complex of small, medium-sized farms. There is little interaction between the two. The work combines an historical overview with an emphasis on relations central to the analysis of forms of agricultural production.

425 **Factors impeding credit use in small-farm households in Bolivia.**
Calvin J. Miller, Jerry R. Ladman. *Journal of Development Studies*, vol. 19, no. 4 (1983), p. 522-38.
Few Bolivian small-farm households use credit, but most would like to borrow. A framework is developed to formulate hypotheses which will identify factors that inhibit credit use. Concludes that obstacles to borrowing are: the size of the farm, transaction costs, native languages, remote locations, and lack of education.

426 **Legume intercrops and weed control in sun-grown coffee plantings in the Bolivian Yungas.**
Lawrence John Janicki. PhD dissertation, University of Florida, Gainesville, Florida. 121p. bibliog.
Smallholder farmers in the Bolivian Yungas can increase production by applying intermediate technology to sun-grown coffee planting if marketing constraints are removed and a just price is received for their product.

427 **Listen to the people: participant-observer evaluation of development projects.**
Lawrence F. Salmen. New York: Oxford University Press, 1987. 149p. bibliog.
The World Bank, which sponsored this volume, is interested in incorporating the people's perspective into project work so as to narrow the gap between professionals involved in these projects and the intended beneficiaries. Methods of attending to cultural and behavioural factors, that is, 'listening to the people,' are espoused here. They are as important to effective development work as are the more widely recognized tools of financial or economic analysis. This book examines two cases-studies; one in La Paz, Bolivia, and a second in Guayaquil, Ecuador. It is arranged in three sections: part one describes and explains the participant-observer, which is, in the case of the La Paz study, a neighbourhood committee; part two describes the place and the projects; and part three explains the mechanics of the participant-observer evaluation. The appendixes provide a step-by-step guide to conducting participant-observer evaluation.

428 **Migration among landholdings by Bolivian *campesinos*.**
Connie Weil. *Geographical Review*, vol. 73, no. 2 (1983), p. 182-97.
Examines the Andean practice of maintaining farmlands in several micro-environments. Such practices developed in pre-Columbian times and gave greater economic security to farming families.

429 **Peasants in transition: the changing economy of the Peruvian Aymará: a general systems approach.**
Theodore C. Lewellen. Boulder, Colorado: Westview Press, 1978, 195p.
A highly readable account of agricultural practices, and social, economic and cultural change among the landholding Aymará peasants.

430 **The well-tempered capitalist: profiles from some Bolivian coops. (Based on a comparative study of four associations of peasant cooperatives).**
Judith Tendler. *Grassroots Development*, vol. 8, no. 2 (1984), p. 37-47. bibliog.
Discusses the real contributions that co-operatives can make to development in the context of an assessment of their propaganda and activities. Co-operatives do limit membership and form élites, but ultimately the environment, and the nature of the tasks they are obliged to perform, determine how benefits are shared.

431 **What to think about cooperatives: a guide from Bolivia.**
Judith Tendler, Kevin Healey, Carol Michales O'Laughlin. *Grassroots Development*, vol. 7, no. 2 (1983), p. 19-38. map. bibliog.
A comparative study of four peasant associations which questions the traditional assumptions about rural co-operatives, and which shows them in a negative light.

432 **Wheat seed marketing in eastern Bolivia.**
Nicholas William Minot. MS thesis, Michigan State University, East Lansing, Michigan, 1985. 168p. bibliog.
An analysis of the economic and organizational aspects of seed industries in various underdeveloped nations, which pays particular attention to the delivery of certified seed. Describes successful reforms in this area in lowland Bolivia.

# Land reform

433 **Agrarian reform and developmental change in Parotani, Bolivia.**
Evelyn K. Clark. PhD dissertation, Indiana University, Bloomington, Indiana, 1970. 263p. bibliog.
Examines the impact of land reform on the former hacienda, Parotani, in the lower Cochabamba valley. Significant development has occurred since 1953. Consumption and savings are studied as well as migration patterns.

434 **Agrarian reform and migration on the Bolivian Altiplano.**
Hans Buechler. PhD dissertation, Columbia University, New
York, 1966. 191p. bibliog.

Studies the impact of land reform and migration on a free community and on an
ex-hacienda. One effect has been the development of a migration community,
which is characterized by the movement of people to and from the city. The
absence of a patron has led to the creation of a new élite of village leaders.

435 **Agrarian reform in Bolivia.**
US Department of State. Washington, DC: US Government
Printing Office, 1962. 6p.

A brief review of the problems facing agrarian reform in Bolivia and the
implications of reform politics for US foreign policy.

436 **Agrarian reform in Latin America.**
Robert J. Alexander. New York: Macmillan, 1974. 118p. bibliog.
(Latin America Series).

A general introduction to agrarian reform in Mexico, Bolivia, Venezuela and
Cuba, which seeks to explain why land reform has become a crucial issue and why
it can no longer be postponed. Alexander studies the role of agrarian reform in
revolution and its ramifications for the United States and the rest of the world.

437 **Agrarian reform in Latin America.**
Royal Institute of International Affairs. London: Oxford
University Press, 1962. 42p.

A brief review of the agrarian reform issue in Latin America, which includes a
section on Bolivia (p. 10-14). Analysis is comparative; other cases discussed
include Mexico, Cuba and Guatemala.

438 **The agrarian reforms of Mexico and Bolivia: a comparison.**
Carlo Geneletti, Wilma Geneletti. *Centro Sociale*, vol. 21 (1974),
p. 3-22, 115-17.

An analysis of the agrarian reform programmes of Mexico and Bolivia (ca. 1960s-
73). In Bolivia the MNR favoured capitalist development of the agrarian sector
where *campesino* input was minimal or non-existent. In areas where peasant
pressure was stronger, the development of capitalist enterprise was non-existent.
The crucial difference between the two cases is that in Mexico changes were
implemented after the peasantry was defeated but in Bolivia the peasant class was
able to continue in its dependent status.

439 **The ambiguity of reform: man and land in highland Bolivia.**
William E. Carter. PhD dissertation, Columbia University, New
York, 1963. 264p. bibliog.

Relates community structure to land use, and to values and attitudes which are
the same both in free communities and on former haciendas. These continue
despite reform.

93

440 **An analysis of the Bolivian land reform by means of a comparison between the Peruvian haciendas and the Bolivian exhaciendas.**
Melvin Burke. PhD dissertation, University of Pittsburgh, Pennsylvania, 1967. 243p. bibliog.

Considers Bolivian land reform in the Lake Titicaca region. The major conclusions are that there has been an increase in land productivity and a decrease in labour productivity, and that capital productivity has not changed.

441 **Aymará communities and the Bolivian agrarian reform.**
William E. Carter. Gainesville, Florida: University of Florida Press, 1965. 89p. maps. (University of Florida Monographs. Social Sciences, no. 24).

Land reform has had an impact on the formal aspects of rural life in Bolivia. However, the Indian continues to live in a subordinate, impoverished social position.

442 **Bolivia and its agrarian reform: a review of recent literature.**
Herbert S. Klein. *Peasant Studies Newsletter*, vol. 5, no. 4 (1976), p. 20-24.

A review of the recent literature pertaining to the process of land reform begun in Bolivia during the 1952 revolution.

443 **Bolivia: the restrained revolution.**
Richard W. Patch. *Annals*, 334 (1964), p. 123-32.

Bolivia's peasants forced agrarian reform on the MNR in 1953. The result has been economically disastrous, but the peasants have been politically integrated into national life. This essay advocates that the United States should extend aid to 'prop up' this democratic revolution.

444 **Bolivia y su reforma agraria.** (Bolivia and its agrarian reform.)
Arturo Urquidi Morales. La Paz: Editorial los Amigos del Libro, 1969. 199p. bibliog.

A history of Bolivia's agrarian structure with a concise summary of the agrarian reform legislation.

445 **Camba: a study of land and society in eastern Bolivia.**
Dwight B. Heath. PhD dissertation, Yale University, New Haven, Connecticut, 1959. 302p. bibliog.

An ethnographic study of an area in eastern Bolivia which describes land tenure systems of the pre- and post-1953 era. Little land has been redistributed and landowners who supported the MNR have not been expropriated; neither has agricultural technology improved nor production figures risen.

446  **A case study of ex-hacienda Toralapa in the Tiraque region of the**
    **upper Cochabamba valley.**
    Joseph F. Dorsey.  Madison, Wisconsin: University of
    Wisconsin–Madison, Land Tenure Center, 1975. 84p. bibliog.
A study of the effects of Bolivian land reform on income, production, education
and socio-economic welfare. The positive results include a more equitable
distribution of food and wages.

447  **Change on the Altiplano: a success story of land reform and**
    **technological innovation in a Bolivian village.**
    Richard W. Patch.  American Universities Field Staff, 1966. 13p.
    (West Coast South America Series, vol. 13, no. 1).
Land reform has profoundly influenced the outlook of the Bolivian peasantry. So
far there have been no concrete results or improvements, but the attitudes of the
peasants and their integration into national life has been achieved.

448  **Compilación legal de la reforma agraria en Bolivia.** (Collection of
    the agrarian reform legislation in Bolivia.)
    La Paz: Editorial 'Fénix', 1955. 336p.
A collection of the laws pertaining to agrarian reform for the 1952-53 period;
including the 1953 laws which created the National Agrarian Reform Service.

449  **Consideraciones de orden doctrinal sobre la reforma agraria en**
    **Bolivia.** (Considerations concerning the ideological issues of
    agrarian reform in Bolivia.)
    Arturo Urquidi Morales.  *Estudios Andinos* (La Paz), vol. 1,
    no. 2 (1961), p. 13-50.
A review of the political and ideological issues of the agrarian reform controversy
over the last one hundred years. Particular attention is paid to the development of
ideology from 1928, when the first principles of agrarian reform were enunciated,
to the passage of the agrarian reform decree in 1953.

450  **The effects of continued landlord presence in the Bolivian**
    **countryside during the post-reform era: lessons to be learned.**
    Peter Graeff.  Madison, Wisconsin: University of
    Wisconsin–Madison, Land Tenure Center, 1974. 36p. bibliog.
Examines the consequences of retaining pre-reform agricultural structures in the
post-revolutionary era.

451 **El feudalismo de Melgarejo y la reforma agraria (proceso de la propiedad territorial y de la política de Bolivia.** (The feudalism of Melgarejo and agrarian reform (property and politics in Bolivia.)) Luis Antezana E. La Paz: the author, 1970. 175p.

General Mariano Melgarejo (president from 1865 to 1871), was responsible for the creation of Bolivia's feudal agrarian structure. The 1952 revolution was an attempt to destroy that feudalism.

452 **El feudalismo en América y la reforma agraria boliviana.** (Feudalism in America and Bolivian agrarian reform.) Arturo Urquidi Morales. Cochabamba: Editorial los Amigos del Libro, 1966. 411p. bibliog.

Traces the development of feudalism in Latin America and the agrarian reform in Bolivia in 1953. The author concludes that the MNR revolution was democratic in nature, and anti-imperialistic and anti-feudal in its tone and ideology.

453 **The hacienda system and agrarian reform in highland Bolivia: a re-evaluation.** Daniel Heyduk. *Ethnology*, vol. 13, no. 1 (1974), p. 71-81.

Rural society in highland Bolivia has undergone a transformation rather than a revolution as the old social order has continued to provide a sub-stratum for the new system. The hacienda system has adapted to the new political, social and economic environment of Bolivia.

454 **The impact of Bolivian agrarian reform on class formation.** U. Mendelberg. *Latin American Perspectives*, vol. 12, no. 3 (summer 1985), p. 45-58. bibliog.

Measures the impact of agrarian reform on the Bolivian peasantry. The results were mixed; peasant status became divided into rich, poor and landless peasants.

455 **Institution building through self-help in rural developing areas: an integrated approach.** Yair Levi. *Centro Sociale*, vol. 21 (1974), p. 261-91.

An early experience in the development of rural self-help institutions is studied in order to demonstrate how community development programmes can be applied to the evaluation of traditional groups in rural areas.

456 **Land reform and economic change in the Yungas.** Madeline B. Leóns. In: *Beyond the Revolution: Bolivia since 1952*. Edited by J. Malloy. Pittsburg, Pennsylvania: University of Pittsburg Press, 1971. 268p. bibliog.

In post-1952 Bolivia the peasant communities of small landholders have replaced the hacienda as a social unit. At the same time mestizo power brokers have replaced the local *hacendado* (landowner). Peasants also exercise power through their syndicates, through participation in the local markets, and through their increased supply of cash.

### 457 Land reform and social revolution in Bolivia.
Dwight B. Heath, Charles J. Erasmus, Hans C. Buechler. New York: Praeger, 1970. 464p. maps. bibliog. (Praeger Special Studies in International Economics and Development).

A book of essays dealing with various issues which are related to the 1952 revolution and the ensuing series of reforms.

### 458 Land reform in Bolivia.
Dwight B. Heath. *Inter-American Economic Affairs*, vol. 12, no. 4 (1959), p. 3-27.

The social and economic impact of the 1953 agrarian reform laws is analysed. Although feudalism has been abolished, few of the other objectives of agrarian reform have been realized. Agrarian reform has not promoted development.

### 459 Land reform in Bolivia; country paper.
Ronald J. Clark. Washington, DC: USAID, 1970. 96p.

A description, analysis and evaluation of Bolivia's agrarian reform. Too much has been expected from the reforms, and this has led to some confusion and inefficiency. The Bolivian government has to meet certain service requirements in the rural areas before improvements can be measured. Despite changes, however, traditional land tenure systems continue.

### 460 Land reform in the Bolivian Yungas.
Madeline Barbara Leóns. *América Indigena* (Mexico City), vol. 27, no. 4 (1967), p. 689-713.

After surveying five ex-haciendas in the Yungas, the author concludes that the small property system has been institutionalized and that the co-operatives have failed.

### 461 Land reform in three communities of Cochabamba, Bolivia.
Marcelo Peinado Sotomayor. PhD dissertation, University of Wisconsin, Madison, 1969. 272p. bibliog.

Describes peasant conditions in pre-1952 Bolivia and the principal changes introduced into the landholding patterns by the agrarian reform. Areas in which there are inadequacies are noted and courses of action are suggested.

### 462 *Minifundia*, productivity and land reform in Cochabamba.
Carlos Camacho Saa. PhD dissertation, University of Wisconsin, Madison, 1967. 179p. bibliog.

Productivity on the post-reform *minifundia* (small landholding) is low, but probably no lower than on the ex-haciendas. This study is based on information gleaned from 142 interviews with inhabitants of Ucureña near Cochabamba.

463 **Peasants and revolution: the case of Bolivia, part I.**
Andrew Pearse. *Economy and Society*, vol. 1, no. 3 (1972),
p. 255-80.
Explains how agrarian serfdom survived in Bolivia up to 1952 and describes the
social control system which maintained it. See also Pearse's 'Peasants and
revolution: the case of Bolivia, part II' (*Economy and Society*, vol. 1, no. 4
(1972), p. 399-424), which studies the agrarian system in the period 1952 to 1972.

464 **The politicization function of agrarian interest groups: a case study
of the Bolivian** *campesino sindicatos.*
Carey G. Rickabaugh. PhD dissertation, University of Maryland,
College Park, Maryland, 1968. 242p. bibliog.
Studies peasant agricultural syndicates as institutions which brought about the
political socialization of the peasantry. These syndicates have achieved one of the
chief goals of the 1952 revolution – the integration of the *campesino* into national
life.

465 **Power, class and rural development in southern Bolivia.**
Kevin J. Healy. PhD dissertation, Cornell University, Ithaca,
New York, 1979. 382p. bibliog.
A micro-study of agrarian élites in relation to the agrarian reform in Bolivia,
(1952-64 period), and rural modernization efforts, (1964-78 period). To
demonstrate the power of the landowning class of the department of Chuquisaca,
numerous examples of counter-reform tactics are included.

466 **Problems and conflicts over land ownership in Bolivia.**
Ronald J. Clark. *Inter-American Economic Affairs*, vol. 22, no. 4
(spring 1969), p. 3-18.
Discusses conflicts over landownership in post-revolutionary Bolivia. The government has been unable to process landownership claims quickly enough and
furthermore, behaviour patterns, especially among the older *campesinos*, have
remained traditional in nature. The three principal conclusions drawn here are:
title distribution could, and should, be done more quickly; all the lands of large
landowners should have been confiscated; and the role of the peasant unions are
important on a local level.

467 **La reforma agraria campesina en Bolivia.** (Peasant agrarian reform
in Bolivia.)
Luis Antezana E. *Revista Mexicana de Sociología*, vol. 31, no. 2
(1969), p. 245-321.
A detailed history of the agrarian conditions which have existed in Bolivia, and
the relationship between these conditions and the national political process. The
account begins in the mid-1800s and briefly discusses the 1952 revolution and
agrarian reform up to 1962.

468 **Report on an agricultural survey in Bolivia.**
Jerusalem: Ministry for Foreign Affairs. Department for
International Cooperation, 1962. 14p.
Recommends a host of changes including improved irrigation, rural instruction,
the creation of regional experimental stations and a veterinary service. Such
reforms, coupled with other changes, would transform Bolivian agriculture and
make it a positive and important factor in economic development.

469 **Revolution and land reform in the Bolivian Yungas of La Paz.**
Katherine Barnes von Marschall. La Paz: Sociedad Nacional de
Reforma Agraria (SNRA), 1970. 233p. bibliog.
A study of the former haciendas of the Yungas area. This volume outlines the
pre-reform land tenure system, traces the reform process and details the new
tenure system introduced as part of the 1952 revolution. The new land tenure
system is studied in its social, political and community dimensions.

470 **Revolution and land reform in Chuquisaca and Potosí.**
Katherine Barnes von Marschall. La Paz: Sociedad Nacional de
Reforma Agraria (SNRA) 1970. 163p. bibliog.
A case-study of agrarian reform in southern Bolivia, and specifically, the
Chuquisaca-Potosí region. The degree of isolation of the haciendas and Indian
communities is an important factor in determining how each has been effected by
agrarian reform. Problems develop when former landowners maintain their
presence in the area after reform has taken place.

471 **Social impliciations of the Bolivian agrarian reform.**
Richard W. Patch. PhD dissertation, Cornell University, Ithaca,
New York, 1955. 292p. bibliog.
Peasants have been conditioned to adopt a passive, conservative viewpoint by the
feudal hacienda structure. Land reform, it is argued, would change such attitudes.

472 **Stratification and pluralism in the Bolivian Yungas.**
Madeline Barbara Leóns. In: *The social anthropology of Latin
America: essays in honor of Ralph Leon Beals.* Edited by Walter
Goldschmidt, Harry Hoijer. Los Angeles, California: University of
California, Latin American Center, 1970, p. 256-82. (Latin
American Studies, no. 14).
A sociological analysis of the impact of land reform on the peasantry of the
Yungas areas near La Paz.

473 **What life after land reform?**
Grace Goodell. *Policy Review*, no. 24 (spring 1983), p. 121-48.
Examines land reform within the context of US foreign policy and discusses how
such a policy provides inexhaustible opportunities for state paternalism. There are
a few references to Bolivia but most of the essay deals with the Third World in a
general way and includes many examples from the Philippines.

# Colonization

474 **Bolivia's developing interior.**
Richard W. Patch.  American University Field Staff, 1962. 13p.
map. (West Coast South America Series, vol. 9, no. 3).

There is a misconception, still held by many, that highland peasants stubbornly resist relocation to far richer agricultural sites in the lowlands and Yungas, the subtropical valleys. Patch, writing in the early 1960s, indicated that planned and spontaneous migration was occurring in Bolivia and argued that within perhaps a generation Bolivia may be thought of as a land of lush tropics. It only required roads and slowly, often by hand, the roads were being built.

475 **Bolivia's experiments in development without aid: a case study of one man's attack on production, processing problems, and marketing.**
Richard W. Patch.  American Universities Field Staff, 1964. 21p.
map. (West Coast South America Series, vol. 11, no. 4).

Examines the contribution of a Bolivian government official and promoter, Alfonso Gumucio Reyes, to the development of the eastern Bolivian province of Santa Cruz.

476 **By hook or by crook: Alfalfa Bill Murray, colonizer in Bolivia.**
Courtney A. Vaughn.  *Journal of the West*, vol. 18, no. 1
(Jan. 1979), p. 67-72.

William Henry, better known as Alfalfa Bill, was an Oklahoma farmer who received a contract from the Bolivian government to develop and settle a 750,000-acre tract of land in eastern Bolivia. The author examines why the government had to terminate the contract in 1925.

477 **Camba and Kolla: migration and development in Santa Cruz, Bolivia.**
Allyn MacLean Stearman.  Orlando, Florida: University of
Central Florida Press, 1985. 227p. bibliog.

The separatist philosophy of the Camba has been maintained since colonial times. This is an excellent analysis of intra-national migration and of the settlement of Santa Cruz by highland people.

478 **Colonization in eastern Bolivia: problems and prospects.**
Allyn MacLean Stearman.  *Human Organization*, vol. 32, no. 3
(1973), p. 285-93.

Examines attempts by the government to redistribute the population of Bolivia away from the densely populated areas of the western highlands to the lightly populated areas of eastern Bolivia. The Bolivian *Oriente* offers vast economic potential.

479　**Colonization policy and peasant economy in the Amazon Basin.**
Frans J. Schuurman.　*Boletín de Estudios Latinoamericanos y del Caribe*, vol. 27, (1979), p. 29-41.

Examines attempts by the governments of Brazil, Bolivia, Peru, Ecuador and Colombia to develop their Amazonian agricultural potential.

480　**Cuenca del Río de la Plata: estudio para su planificación y desarrollo.** (Basin of the River Plate: a planning and development study.)
Washington, DC: Organization of American States (OAS), 1974. 166p. maps.

Part of a study of the Bermejo and Pilcomayo rivers undertaken by the Argentine and Bolivian governments with the aid of the regional development office of the OAS. The commission was established in order to explore the possibility of developing hydro-electric power and how such power would be regulated.

481　**Eastern Bolivia: the white promised land.**
Norman Lewis.　Copenhagen: International Secretariat of IWGIA, 1978. 27p. map. (International Work Group for Indigenous Affairs Document, 31).

Examines the impact on the Indian population of the Bolivian government's attempt to attract white settlers, particularly from Rhodesia, South Africa and South West Africa. Historically, Bolivia has been unsuccessful in attracting white immigrants.

482　**From resource frontier to periphery: agricultural colonization east of the Andes.**
Frans J. Schuurman.　*Tijdschrift voor Economische en Sociale Geografie*, vol. 69 (1978), p. 95-104. map. bibliog.

Examines land settlement patterns in Bolivia, Colombia, Ecuador and Peru.

483　**Government, *campesinos*, and business in the Bolivian Chapare: a case study of Amazonian occupation.**
Connie Weil, Jim Weil.　*Inter-American Economic Affairs*, vol. 36, no. 4 (spring 1983), p. 29-62. maps. bibliog.

Examines the effects of colonization on the people and environment in the Chapare. Agricultural colonization was promoted by the 1953 reforms in order to solve some social and economic problems. Peasants establish unions in new areas and practice slash-and-burn agriculture. Although nutritional levels are adequate, colonizers still need potable water and waste disposal systems.

484 **The highland migrant in lowland Bolivia: multiple resource migration and the horizontal archipelago.**
Allyn MacLean Stearman. *Human Organization.* (Society for Applied Anthropology), vol. 37, no. 2 (summer 1978), p. 181-85.
Discusses the vertical exploitation of environmental resources in the Andean highlands and demonstrates how this concept is used to explain the multiple economic activities practiced by recent highland colonists of the Santa Cruz region of eastern Bolivia.

485 **Investment in access roads and spontaneous colonization, additional evidence from Bolivia.**
E. G. Wennergren. *Land Economics*, vol. 52, no. 1 (1976), p. 88-95.
Spontaneous settlement along new roadways indicates that colonists respond positively when economic opportunities are put before them.

486 **Migration among landholdings by Bolivian *campesinos*.**
Connie Weil. *Geographical Review*, vol. 73, no. 2 (1983), p. 182-97.
Demonstrates that the migration in the Chapare colonization zone is not a simple movement from one place to another but involves the maintenance of multiple holdings with different ecological characteristics. In the community of Muluzama property owners spend twenty-five per cent of their time away from their land.

487 **Peasants, entrepreneurs, and social change: frontier development in lowland Bolivia.**
Lesley Gill. Boulder, Colorado: Westview Press, 1987. 246p. bibliog.
Measures the benefits of migration and colonization programmes and how they affect socio-economic change and bring about integration.

488 **Pioneering as an ecological process: a model and test case of frontier adaptation.**
Edited by David W. Hess, William W. Savage, Jr., Stevens I. Thompson. *The Frontier: Comparative Studies*, vol. 2 (1979), p. 123-51. bibliog.
Examines the colonization of the Santa Cruz region, an isolated and lightly populated area of lowland eastern Bolivia, in the light of the authors' theory of settlement.

489 **Política de desarrollo regional en el oriente boliviano.** (Politics of regional development in eastern Bolivia.)
Ulbrich Reye. Bilbao, Spain: Ediciones Deusto, 1970. 194p. maps. bibliog.
An excellent introduction to the potential for economic development in the

eastern sections of Bolivia. The author examines the cultural, demographic and economic aspects of the Bolivian national effort to populate this rich area. This work is essentially a descriptive study.

490 **Political penetration and conflict resolution in the Bolivian Yungas.**
Madeline Barbara Leóns. *Journal of Developing Areas*, vol. 18, no. 4 (July 1984), p. 465-80. bibliog.

Examines how peasants use traditional and newly acquired political and legal skills to solve conflicts in modern Bolivia. However, the state's ability to mold village life is a strong but subtle power.

491 **Santa Cruz: a study of economic growth in eastern Bolivia.**
G. Richard Fletcher. *Inter-American Economic Affairs*, vol. 29, no. 2 (autumn 1975), p. 23-41.

Surveys the economic growth of Santa Cruz since 1825 with an emphasis on the effects of central government policy on economic development.

492 **The search for a series of small successes: frontiers of settlement in eastern Bolivia.**
J. Valerie Fifer. *Journal of Latin American Studies*, vol. 14, no. 2 (1982), p. 407-32. bibliog.

A noted British geographer examines Bolivian attempts to colonize the eastern frontier region. The article reviews the several plans which have been introduced to promote: spontaneous colonization, guided colonization and highly directed colonization, including some with contractual obligations. The area measures about 1.4 million square kilometres and contains about 250,000 people.

493 **A South American odyssey.**
Michael Morgan. *Américas* (OAS), vol. 31, no. 10 (Oct. 1979), p. 28-34.

Traces the steps of William Wright through the territories of Argentina, Chile, Bolivia and Peru from 1912-13. Wright, an employee of the Department of Agriculture of the United States was searching for the origins of the white potato.

494 **South America's marginal highway.**
Hernán Horna. *Journal of Developing Areas*, vol. 10, no. 4 (1976), p. 409-24.

Fernando Belaúnde Terry, president of Peru between 1963 and 1968, encouraged far-reaching developments in the infrastructure in the form of a 3,720-mile road to connect Venezuela, Colombia, Ecuador, Peru and Bolivia. The project has succeeded in opening millions of acres of land for colonization whilst, at the same time, promoting the geographical, political and economic integration of the nations of South America. The project is set for completion in 1995.

# Japanese colonization

495 **Agricultural practices and household organization in a Japanese pioneer community of lowland Bolivia.**
Hiroski Kashiwazaki. *Human Ecology*, vol. 11, no. 3 (1983), p. 283-319.

Describes the colonization carried out by Japanese pioneers in Bolivia. Tests two hypotheses: that pioneer agriculture stimulates the formation of large family households to cope with an assumed labour shortage; and that variation in household organization produces variations in agricultural practices. Data does not suggest that large family households are formed. It does, however, indicate that changes in household composition influence the amount of land farmed and the level of mechanization in agriculture.

496 **Changes in family and household organization in an overseas Japanese pioneer community.**
Stephen I. Thompson. *Journal of Comparative Family Studies*, vol. 2, no. 2 (1971), p. 165-77.

A community study of a Japanese pioneer colony in San Juan Yapacani, Bolivia. It has been hypothesized that the availability of large amounts of land would result in the fragmentation and breakdown of traditional family life. This has not happened and the traditional Japanese family structure has adapted and survived in frontier conditions.

497 **Emigration and remigration of Okinawans settled in the lowlands of eastern Bolivia in relation to background characteristics of their place of origin.**
Hiroski Kashiwazaki, Tsuguyoski Suzuki. *Human Ecology*, vol. 6, no. 1 (1977), p. 3-14.

Studies Japanese immigration to eastern Bolivia and attempts to determine which settler is likely to remain in a pioneering area and why.

498 **Fertility pattern of Japanese agricultural settlers in eastern Bolivia.**
Hiroski Kashiwazaki. *Journal of Biosocial Science*, vol. 9, no. 1 (1977), p. 53-60. bibliog.

Compares the fertility of Japanese immigrants to Bolivia with those in southern Brazil and with the Japanese in their homeland. The study is based on a 1974 survey of 78 households and interviews with 106 married women. The fertility of the Japanese immigrant to Bolivia is high when compared with the data from Japan and Brazil. Fertility rates correlate with the level current in Japan when the individual left the homeland.

499   **Japanese settlement in eastern Bolivia and Brazil.**
      James L. Tigner.   *Journal of Interamerican Studies and World Affairs*, vol. 24, no. 4 (Nov. 1982), p. 496-517. bibliog.
Reviews major studies on Japanese immigration. Bolivia does not incorporate the Japanese into its social system whilst Brazil does. The study is based on government documents from three nations.

# Trade and Industry

500 **Allocation of industry in the Andean Common Market.**
Jan Wengel.   The Hague: Martinus Nijhoff, 1980. 177p. bibliog.
(Studies in Development and Planning, 11).
The objective of this text is to develop and implement a model for allocating the
industries of the Sectorial Programmes of Industrial Development in the Andean
Common Market. One of the main problems to be resolved in integration
schemes among less developed countries is that of the distribution of the resulting
benefits. The problem of allocating industries to the member countries, while
taking into account their particular distributional constraints, is not difficult in
theory. In this book, an integer programming model is formulated, based on the
investment criterion developed by Bruno and Krueger (the domestic resource cost
of foreign exchange), and the Corden measure of the effective rate of protection.
The model, which circumvents the usual data problems, is then implemented to
allocate the industries of the Petrochemical Programme of the Andean Common
Market.

501 **Bolivia exporta; directorio de exportadores y notas sobre la
economía boliviana.** (Bolivia exports; directory of exporters and
notes about the Bolivian economy.)
Ministerio de Industria y Comercio (Bolivia).   La Paz: Ministerio
de Industria y Comercio, 1972. 252p.
A list of export houses with a general introduction concerning business opportunities and information about how to conduct business in Bolivia.

502 **Bolivia: problems of a pre- and post-revolutionary export economy.**
Walter Gómez.   *Journal of Developing Areas*, vol. 10, no. 4
(1976), p. 461-84.
Bolivian dependence on the export of a single commodity, tin, is typical of an

106

underdeveloped economy. During the early 20th century mining profits were very high and taxes very low. The railway system benefited only the mineowners and exacerbated the nation's economic dualism. After the 1952 revolution and the nationalization of the tin industry, the government mining corporation took over operation of the mines, and production levels declined sharply. Private mining failed to stimulate general economic development and post-revolutionary taxation damaged the mining sector.

503 **Butchers, bribes, and bandits: market relations in Cochabamba, Bolivia (game theory (application), network analysis (application of), Latin American studies, coalitions).**
Erica Gail Polakoff.    PhD dissertation, Cornell University, Ithaca, New York, 1985. 243p. bibliog.
Market relations and strategies are analysed from two perspectives. Network analysis provides a structural view of the market; game theory provides an understanding of market processes.

504 **Conduct and code: an analysis of market syndicates and social revolutions in La Paz, Bolivia.**
Hans Buechler, Judith-Maria Buechler.    In: *Ideology and social change in Latin America.* Edited by June Nash, Juan Corradi. New York: Gordon & Breach, 1977. 305p. bibliog.
The formation of market syndicates, or market unions, in La Paz was a consequence of the agrarian reform decree of 1953. Syndicates mediate between the city government and the vendors, seeking to prevent graft and abuse. Grouped into federations and into larger confederations, the leadership is democratically elected. In 1974, the unions' activities were suspended and leadership was co-opted by the government.

505 **Efecto de las exportaciones norteamericanas de trigo en Bolivia, Perú, Ecuador y Colombia.** (The effect of North American exports of wheat in Bolivia, Peru, Ecuador and Colombia.)
Mario Valderrama.    Bogotá, Colombia: *Estudios Rurales Latinoamericanos*, vol. 2, no. 2 (May-Aug. 1979), p. 173-98. bibliog.
A very interesting survey of the impact of the international grain trade on underdeveloped nations. Rural countries such as Bolivia come to rely on cheap imported foodstuffs and allow their own capacity to decline.

506 **Industrialization and regional planning in Bolivia.**
Wolfgang Schoop.    Amsterdam: Interuniversitair Centrum voor Studie en Documentatie van Latijns Amerika, 1978. 13p. maps. bibliog.
Discusses a new law concerning regional development corporations of Bolivia

with special reference to Santa Cruz and the 1976-80 five-year plan. Maps of centres of planned industrial development in Bolivia are also included.

507 **Las inversiones extranjeras en el sector de hidrocarburos.** (Foreign investment in the hydrocarbon sector.)
Julio Prudencio B.   La Paz: Centre do Información y Documentación de Bolivia (CIDOB), 1979. 73p.

This document explains the relationship between the international oil companies and Bolivia. It concentrates on the activities of Standard Oil, and Bolivian Gulf Oil, and concludes that Bolivian oil legislation does not adequately protect natural resources from foreign exploitation.

508 **Market processes in La Paz, Bolivia.**
Charles Slater (et al.).   East Lansing, Michigan: Latin American Studies Centre, Michigan State University, 1969. 242p.

A first attempt to describe and evaluate the exchange processes for consumer goods and food in La Paz. This AID-related project had a special interest in the food marketing system, together with peasants' participation in the marketing system.

509 **Marketing in Bolivia.**
Richard F. Muenzer.   Washington, DC: Domestic and International Business Administration, 1977. 32p. bibliog.

Provides information about marketing overseas.

510 **Oil and politics in Latin America: nationalist movements and state companies.**
George D. E. Philip.   Cambridge: Cambridge University Press, 1982. 577p. bibliog. (Cambridge Latin American Studies, no. 40).

A very useful introduction to the politics of oil in modern Latin America. Includes a section on Bolivian oil and trade relations with energy-poor Brazil and Argentina.

# Mining

511  **La administración empírica de las minas nacionalizadas.**
(Provisional administration of the nationalized mines.)
René Ruiz González.   La Paz: Librería y Editorial 'Juventud',
1980. 2nd ed. 322p. maps. bibliog.

Dr. Ruiz González combines historical and statistical information with an
administrative analysis and an evaluation of the physiological forces which have
brought about dramatic changes in the mining industry in Bolivia. The volume is
organized into five sections: the first three examine the origins and significance of
mining to Bolivian national development; section four deals with the system
developed by the government to operate the mines after expropriation occurred;
and the final part describes military intervention in the mines.

512  **Allocative and x-efficiency in state-owned mining enterprises –
comparisons between Bolivia and Indonesia.**
Malcolm Gillis.   *Journal of Comparative Economics*, vol. 6, no. 1
(1982), p. 1-23.

Deals with efficiency issues in state-owned enterprises which are involved with
mining minerals in Bolivia and Indonesia. Welfare losses from inefficiency in the
system of allocation appear to be of some importance.

513  **Bolivia – the price of tin.**
Norman Gall.   Hanover, New Hampshire: American Universities
Field Staff, 1974. 13p. (West Coast South America Series, vol. 21,
no.1).

Part one, 'The Patiño mines and enterprises', recounts the story of the Siglo XX
tin mine, which played an important role in the contemporary history of Bolivia.
The opening of the mine marked the beginning of the worldwide economic
activities of the Patiño family. Traces the development of the mine through to its

109

becoming a thoroughly modern economic enterprise, and outlines the career of Simón Ituri Patiño (1862-1947). Part two, 'The crisis of nationalization' (Norman Gall. Hanover, New Hampshire: American Universities Field Staff, 1974. 21p. West Coast South America Series, vol. 21, no. 2) describes the period after 1929, when the mines experienced a decline in production. The present nationalization of the industry, the result of political and social factors, has created mines run by peasant co-operatives and worked by pre-industrial technology.

### 514 Bolivian mining.

Ricardo A. Godoy. *Latin American Research Review*, vol. 20, no. 1 (1985), p. 272-77.

Emphasizes the existing social conditions in Bolivian mining zones, but does not examine mining as an economic activity.

### 515 Breve historia de la minería en Bolivia. (Brief history of mining in Bolivia.)

Walter Hermosa Virreira. La Paz: Editorial los Amigos del Libro, 1979. 218p. bibliog. (Enciclopedia Boliviano).

This history of Bolivian mining is divided into four periods: pre-Columbian, colonial, 19th century and 20th century. The first three chapters give a general overview of silver mining, whilst the latter chapters deal with tin mining, focusing on nationalization, mineral reserves, and the structure of the tin industry.

### 516 The creation of the Patiño tin empire.

Herbert S. Klein. *Inter-American Economic Affairs*, vol. 19, no. 2 (1965), p. 3-24.

A biography of Latin America's most successful entrepreneur and creator of the first multinational corporation in South America. Simón Ituri Patiño, a *cholo* (of mixed blood), was born in modest circumstances in 1860. He began working in the tin industry in the 1880s, bought his first mine in 1894 and, by the 1910s, had emerged as the dominant figure in the Bolivian tin industry. He rapidly expanded his business overseas, purchasing smelting and processing facilities in Britain and the United States. At the time of his death, in 1947, he was the head of a great international tin cartel and one of the most powerful businessmen in the world.

### 517 The economics of tin mining in Bolivia.

Mahmood Ali Ayub, Hideo Hashimoto. Washington, DC: World Bank, 1985. 106p. bibliog.

This scholarly study brings together reliable and consistent data on the Bolivian tin mining sector and analyses the development of the industry from an historical perspective. It is arranged into eight chapters and addresses such issues as: (1) the impact of tin mining on the Bolivian economy; (2) tin pricing and competitiveness; (3) problems of the national mining corporation, COMIBOL; (4) the smelting process; and (5) the tax structure. The study concludes on a pessimistic note and suggests that the best that can be done is to maintain production at the present level, evaluate the tin-producing potential of the lowlands, and diversify into other metals.

518 **Like moonlight on snow: the life of Simón Ituri Patiño.**
John Hewlett. New York: R. M. McBride, 1947. 292p.
This romantic biography, written to commemorate Patiño's death, portrays him as
one of Spanish America's greatest modern heroes.

519 **Patiño, the tin king.**
Charles F. Geddes. London: Robert Hale, 1972. 416p. bibliog.
A readable biography of this remarkable tin baron of Aymará ancestry.

520 **Taxation and mining: nonfuel minerals in Bolivia and other
countries.**
Malcolm Gillis (et al.). Cambridge, Massachusetts: Ballinger
Press, 1978. 358p. bibliog.
A book of nine essays concerning the tax structure as it affects mining. The
Bolivian mining complex is the central focus and Gillis compares mining taxes in
Bolivia with seventeen other nations.

521 **Technical and economic efficiency of peasant miners in Bolivia.**
R. A. Godoy. *Economic Development and Cultural Change*,
vol. 34, no. 1 (Oct. 1985), p. 103-20. bibliog.
Peasant mining creates about three times more employment than mechanized
mining in Bolivia. Peasant miners, using traditional methods, at least 500 years
old, are technically efficient in recovery rates, bleeding the ore to the last drop of
metal.

522 **Tin and the Bolivian economy.**
David John Fox. London: Latin American Publications Fund,
1970. 25p. maps. bibliog.
A concise overview of the tin industry as the cornerstone of the Bolivian
economy. It discusses where the mines are located, their physical structure, the
smelting process, how tin production is organized and lists the problems facing the
industry, including market conditions.

# Social Conditions

## General

523 **Adaption of Aymará and Quechua to the bicultural social context of the Bolivian mines.**
John Hickman, Jack Brown. *Human Organization* (Society for Applied Anthropology), vol. 30, no. 4 (1971), p. 359-66.
A study of acculturation in a bi-cultural setting.

524 **Aggression and hypoglycemia among the Qolla: a study in psycho-biological anthropology.**
Ralph Bolton. *Ethnology*, vol. 12, no. 3 (July 1973), p. 227-58.
Studies why the Qolla Indians of Peru and Bolivia are aggressive in their behaviour. This is a revised version of the author's *Aggression and hypoglycemia among the Qolla* (Claremont, California: Pomono College, Department of Anthology, 1971. 61p. bibliog.).

525 **Agriculture and the supernatural: a case, the Altiplano.**
Richard W. Patch. Hanover, New Hampshire: American Universities Field Staff, 1971. 17p. (West Coast South America Series, vol. 18, no. 4).
Near Lake Titicaca, Aymará-speaking peasants practise subsistence agriculture. Supernatural beliefs impose order on their uncertain existence and are important elements of highland agriculture.

112

526 **Andean kinship and marriage.**
Ralph Bolton, Enrique Mayer. Washington, DC: American
Anthropological Association, 1977. 298p. maps. bibliog.

A book of essays by noted Andean anthropologists, which had previously been
circulated privately among scholars. Essays include: Bernard Lambert's
'Bilaterality in the Andes', (p. 1-27); William E. Carter's 'Trial marriage in the
Andes'; Ralph Bolton's 'The Qolla marriage process', (p. 217-35); William T.
Stuart's and John M. Hickman's 'Descent, alliance and moiety in Chucuito,
Peru – an explanatory sketch of Aymará social organization (p. 43-59); and
Norman Long's 'Commerce and kinship in the Peruvian highland' (p. 153-76). A
section entitled 'References cited' represents an important bibliographical tool.

527 **Bolivia: transplanting apartheid.**
James Goff. *NACLA'S Latin America & Empire Report*, vol. 11,
no. 6 (July-Aug. 1977), p. 28-29.

Bolivia, which has always had difficulty in attracting white immigrants, has
permitted white South Africans to move into eastern regions. This contribution is
more of a note than an analysis of the situation.

528 **Change in the Altiplano.**
Richard W. Patch. Hanover, New Hampshire: American
Universities Field Staff, 1966. 13p. (East Coast South America
Series, vol. 13, no. 1).

A success story of land reform and technological innovation in a Bolivian village.
Pairumani represents such a remarkable achievement because the reforms have
produced changes in attitudes which make innovation and initiative possible.
These changes, unimpressive to the statistical economist, are fundamental for the
transformation of a dependent passive population into an independent and active
population.

529 **Changing rural society; a study of communities in Bolivia.**
William John McEwen. New York: Oxford University Press,
1975. 463p.

Based on the report of a team of field researchers, this study focuses on the
human consequences that followed the economic, political, educational and other
reform measures which were implemented nationally. Six rural communities,
which differed widely in their involvement with the reform programme, were
examined in detail and their residents were observed and interviewed over
periods of several months. The discussion centres on community status and
power, on social stratification and politicization.

530 **Charazani.**
Richard W. Patch. Hanover, New Hampshire: American
Universities Field Staff, 1971. 10p. (West Coast South America
Series, vol. 18, no. 5).

Charazani, a remote Bolivian mountain area, is home to the Callaway Indians
who are famous healers, diviners, witches and experts in the supernatural.

113

531 **The cultural context of courtship and betrothal in a Quechua community of Cochabamba, Bolivia.**
Jaime Luis Daza. PhD dissertation, University of California, Los Angeles, 1983. 132p. bibliog.
Concerns aspects of courtship and betrothal and how it shapes the family. It is based on research conducted in Ucuchi near Cochabamba.

532 **To defend ourselves; ecology and ritual in an Andean village.**
Billie Jean Isbell. Austin, Texas: University of Texas Press, 1978. 289p.
An examination of the role of ritual in a traditional peasant community in highland Bolivia.

533 **Dependency and the failure of feedback: the case of the Bolivian mining communities.**
June Nash. *International Congress of Americanists. Proceedings,* XL. Roma-Geneva, vol. 3 (1972), p. 511-31. bibliog.
The livelihood of Bolivian miners is characterized by dependency in many areas, including job dependency, union dependency and consumer dependency. These are built into caste-like relationships between Indians, *cholos*, and whites. Positions of dominance are maintained through the use of force and also by playing on the vulnerabilities of workers. So long as conditions remain as they are, the author argues, workers will not be able to change their situation.

534 **Explotación agraria y resistencia campesina.** (Agrarian exploitation and peasant resistance.)
Brooke Larson. Cochabamba: Ediciones CERES, 1983. 214p. bibliog.
A collection of five essays on agrarian conditions in Cochabamba from the 18th century to the present.

535 **Huayrapampa: Bolivian highland peasants and the new social order.**
Daniel Heyduk. PhD dissertation, Cornell University, Ithaca, New York, 1971. 308p. bibliog.
The land reform of 1952-53 failed to a great extent to achieve its primary goal, which was the integration of the peasant into the main stream of national life.

536 **The La Paz census of 1970 and attitudes toward sex, reproduction and contraception in Bolivia and Peru.**
Richard W. Patch. Hanover, New Hampshire. American Universities Field Staff, 1970. 10p. (West Coast South America Series, vol. 17, no. 11).
As the birth rate in Bolivia and Peru approached its peak, the rate of population increase has been checked almost exclusively by infant mortality. With recent

massive technological development, however, these nations may be only a generation away from the Malthusian nightmare.

537 **Land and labor in the Titicaca basin: an ethnohistory of a highland Aymará community.**
Karen M. Poe. PhD dissertation, University of Virginia, Charlottesville, Virginia, 1979. 303p. bibliog.
Emphasizes the structural evolution of the native community through five centuries of subordination to external forces. Poe combines ethnohistorical and ethnographic data concerning the Aymará Indians of the province of Ingavi with data from the 19th and 20th centuries. The latter focuses on demographic, economic and social change in the community of Sapana and puts this into a national context.

538 **Low classness or wavering populism. A peasant movement in Bolivia.**
Jorge Dandler. In: *Ideology and social change in Latin America*. Edited by June Nash, Juan Corradi. New York: Gordon & Breach, 1977. 305p. bibliog.
Using Cochabamba as a case-study, the author demonstrates the inadequacy of existing theory for correctly analysing peasant participation in politics.

539 **Myth and ideology in the Andean highlands.**
June Nash. In: *Ideology and social change in Latin America*. Edited by June Nash, Juan Corradi. New York: Gordon & Breach, 1977, p. 6-32. 305p. bibliog.
Traces the ideological progression in the consciousness of Bolivian peasants. The author examines a host of pre-conquest and post-conquest indigenous heroes and sees continuity and links between the Oruro carnival heroes and the folk heroes of the 1942 Catavi mine massacre.

540 **The national community development program in Bolivia, and the utilization of Peace Corps volunteers.**
G. F. Baumann. *Community Development Journal*, vol. 5, no. 4 (1970), p. 191-96.
A critical review of the role of the Peace Corps in a developing country.

541 **New patrons for old: changing patron-client relationships in the Bolivian Yungas.**
Dwight B. Heath. *Ethnology*, vol. 12, no. 1 (1973), p. 75-98.
Studies the social and economic aspects of revolutionary change in the Yungas area of Bolivia. In the post-revolutionary era (post-1952) the former *campesinos* have become freeholders, and the new patrons have adapted themselves to changing roles.

542 **A note on Bolivia and Peru.**
Richard W. Patch. Hanover, New Hampshire: American
Universities Field Staff, 1962. 41p. bibliog. (West Coast South
America Series, vol. 9, no. 4).

Provides notes on some of the social, political and economic aspects of these two
Andean nations. The case of Bolivia illustrates that reform is possible, within a
democratic framework, but also that reform leads to disorganization, depression
and frustration.

543 **Panorama de la situación indígena en Paraguay: Quechuas,
Aymarás, Guaraníes, Chulupíes, Tobas, Kollas, Maquiritares,
Parixis y Matacos.** (Panorama of the Indian's situation in
Paraguay: Quechuas, Aymarás, Guaraníes, Chulupíes, Tobas,
Kollas, Maquiritares, Parixis and Matacos.)
Julia Báez. *Casa de las Américas*, vol.16, no. 95 (March-April
1976), p. 66-74.

In October 1974, a congress of Indian representatives was convened in Paraguay.
Twenty-three delegates represented the native peoples of the Americas, including
Bolivia. The convention dealt with major problems confronting today's Indian
population, such as economic exploitation, loss of land and the destruction of
Indian cultures.

544 **Peasants, revolution, and drinking: interethnic drinking patterns in
two Bolivian communities.**
Dwight B. Heath. *Human Organization* (Society for Applied
Anthropology), vol. 30, no. 2 (summer 1971), p. 179-86.

A study of ritualistic drinking and its social effects among Bolivian *campesinos*.

545 **Pluralism and mobility in a Bolivian highland community.**
William Leóns, E. Dorado. Greely, Colorado: University of
Northern Colorado, *Muso*, vol. 2, no. 3 (1977), p. 36-50. bibliog.

Defends pluralism as a social science model for interpreting Bolivian material
from the Chicaloma district, in the southern Yungas.

546 **Rural development in southern Bolivia.**
Kevin J. Healy. PhD dissertation, Cornell University, Ithaca,
New York, 1979. 389p. bibliog.

Describes the role of rural élites in the development process in contemporary
Chuquisaca. This study also surveys events in the region after the 1952 revolution.

547 **Toward a theory of postrevolutionary social change: a six nation comparative study.**
M. T. Naimi. PhD dissertation, Washington State University, Pullman, Washington, DC, 1985. 470p.

A comprehensive comparison of social change between three nations which have experienced social revolution and three developing nations which have not. The author finds that in nations which have experienced revolutions there tends to be an improvement in the distribution of social capital, because agrarian and educational reforms are adopted. However, these revolutionary reforms are seen to be least effective in the area of female benefits.

548 **Trial marriage in the Andes.**
William Carter. In: *Andean kinship and marriage*. Ralph Bolton, Enrique Mayer. Washington, DC: American Anthropological Association, 1977, p. 177-216. bibliog.

This study suggests that trial marriage is not a trial period but a part of an inter-locking series of rituals which seal marriage and kinship bonds.

549 **We eat the mines and the mines eat us: dependency and exploitation in Bolivian tin mines.**
Edited by June Nash. New York: Columbia University Press, 1979. 363p. bibliog.

A highly dramatic and interesting investigation of living conditions and family life in Bolivia's mining areas. The study is based upon a year and a half of filmed research and puts flesh on the skeleton of dependency theory.

550 **Wealth and family background in the occupational career: theory and cross-cultural data.**
Jonathan Kelley. *British Journal of Sociology*, vol. 29, no. 1 (1978), p. 94-109.

Asserts that being a member of a family with high status benefits an individual throughout his life. Studies were conducted at African and Latin American locations, including Bolivia.

# Women

551 **El comité de amas de casa del siglo XX: an organizational experience of Bolivian women.**
Moema Viezzer. *Latin American Perspectives*, vol. 6, no.3 (summer 1970), p. 80-86.

Explains how the Housewives' Committee came into existence and describes the forms of action and struggle. The struggle of the women in mining areas is distinct from the middle class feminist movement. In order to succeed, they must simultaneously approach the questions of class and sex.

552 **Factories and families: urban working women in La Paz, Bolivia (economic development, Latin America).**
Valerie Anne Estes. PhD dissertation, University of California, Berkeley, 1984. 169p. map. bibliog.

An ethnographic account of the work and family roles of Third World women which focuses on women in the domestically-financed food processing factory in La Paz.

553 **Let me speak!: Testimony of Domitila, a woman of the Bolivian mines.**
Domitila Barrios de Chungara, Moema Viezzer. New York: Monthly Review Press, 1979, 235p.

An interview with a woman involved in the women's protest movement in the Bolivian mining areas. Domitila Barrios de Chungara is the wife of a tin miner; she is also the leader and organizer of the Houswives' Committee of the Siglo XX mine.

554 **La libertad: a women's cooperative in highland Bolivia.**
Robert Wasserstrom. *Grassroots Development*, vol. 6, no. 1 (1982), p. 7-12.

The IAF supports a savings and loan co-operative in Cochabamba. Most of its members are women who sell goods in the central market of the city, the focal point of commerce in the region.

555 **The maternal kin unit in Bolivian urban adaptation.**
Gordon Keller. *International Journal of Women's Studies*, vol. 6, no. 4 (1983), p. 336-51.

Examines some basic changes in the structure, functions and values of the traditional peasant family in Cochabamba, Bolivia, which result from rural-urban migration and urban adaptation. In this process the role of the female is crucial, for, as the family unit breaks down she assumes more economic responsibilities.

556 **Resistance and protest: women in the struggle of Bolivia's tin mining communities.**
June Nash. In: *Women cross-culturally: change and challenge*. Edited by Ruby Rohrich-Leavitt. The Hague: Mouton, 1973, p. 261-71. bibliog.

The style and the short-lived glories of the women's labour protest movement act to prevent the outbreak of violence. The women's resistance is admired and considered just, although such behaviour is seen to be abnormal in periods of industrial tranquility.

557  **Something funny happened on the way to the Agora: a comparison of Bolivian and Spanish Galician female migrants.**
Judith-Maria Buechler.  *Anthropological Quarterly*, vol. 49, no. 1 (1976), p. 62-68. bibliog.
Studies the economic activity both of female migrants and of women left behind in an area where there is a high rate of male exodus.

558  **The triple struggle: peasant women in Latin America.**
Audrey Bronstein.  Boston, Massachusetts: South End Press, 1982. 270p. bibliog.
Examines the struggle of Latin American peasant women against the difficulties of underdevelopment, poverty and sexism. The Bolivian section can be found on p. 79-99.

559  **Women and cooperative labor.**
Inge Maria Harman.  Cambridge, Massachusetts: *Cultural Survival Quarterly*, vol. 8, no. 2 (1984), p. 38-40.
A brief discussion of women's role in Bolivian co-operatives. In the Yuras of southern Bolivia the value attached to women's work promotes sexual equality.

# Coca

560  **Carnival and coca leaf; some traditions of the Peruvian Quechua *ayllu*.**
Douglas F. Gifford, Pauline F. Hoggarth.  New York: St. Martin's Press, 1976. 111p. bibliog.
Asserts that primitive societies with 'backward' living conditions are, in fact, highly organized in their behaviour patterns and traditional culture. This study investigates the carnival celebrations of the peasants, the election of local officials and the ritual importance of alcohol and coca consumption.

561  **Coca and popular medicine in Peru: an historical analysis of attitudes.**
Joseph A. Galiano.  In: *Medical anthropology.* Edited by Francis X. Grollig, Harold B. Haley. The Hague: Mouton, 1976, p. 49-66. 485p. bibliog.
An analysis of folk medicine in the highland areas of Peru, which is also applicable to Bolivia.

562 **Coca chewing and high-altitude stress: a spurious correlation.**
Warwick Bray, Colin Dollery. *Current Anthropology*, vol. 24
no. 3 (June 1983), p. 269-82.

Challenges the premise that coca chewing is connected with the rigours of high-altitude life. Ethnohistorical and archaeological evidence suggests that coca was widely used throughout the area before the European conquest, so the benefits of chewing coca are not altitude specific but of a general kind.

563 **Coca chewing: a new perspective.**
Roderick Burchard. In: *Cannabis and culture.* Edited by Vera
Rubin. The Hague: Mouton, 1975, p. 463-84. 568p. bibliog.

Proposes that cocaine models are inadequate for studying and measuring the effects of coca chewing. Given the importance of the coca-chewing custom among the undernourished population of the Andes, this topic requires additional study. This essay also appears in *Current Anthropology*, vol. 21, no. 1 (1980), p. 108–09.

564 **Coca in Bolivia**
Robert B. South. *Geographical Review*, vol. 67, no. 1 (1977),
p. 22-23.

Explores the national use of coca by the peasant classes of Bolivia. This custom is allegedly on the decline because the international demand for cocaine has driven the cost of coca beyond the means of most peasants.

565 **Coca in the historical development of Bolivia.**
Roberto Choque Canqui. In: *Traditional use of the coca leaf in
Bolivia: multidisciplinary study, final report.* La Paz: Museo
Nacional de Etnografía y Folklore. 1978, p. 151-58.

A brief introductory survey to the traditional uses of the coca plant in Andean culture, traditions and medicine.

566 **Traditional use of coca in Bolivia.**
William E. Carter, Mauricio Mamani P. La Paz: Museo Nacional
de Etnografía y Folklore, 1978. 269p. bibliog.

A random sample of 2,991 households in highland areas suggests that the amount of coca needed for traditional consumers is greater than production estimates at the time of the study.

# Health

567 **La alimentación en el Tawantinsuyu.** (Diet in Tawantinsuyu.)
Santiago E. Antúnez de Mayolo R. *Etnohistoria y Antropología Andina*, vol. 1 (1978), p. 277-98.
Concludes that the traditional Andean diet is healthy. The study is based on extensive documentation and research.

568 **Altitude and infant growth in Bolivia: a longitudinal study.**
J. D. Haas (et al.). *American Journal of Physical Anthropology*, vol. 59, no. 3 (Nov. 1982), p. 251-62. bibliog.
Analyses the growth of 79 babies over their first year of life to determine the relationship between altitude and human development.

569 **De los árboles, frutos, plantas y otras cosas medicinales que tiene este reyno.** (Of trees, fruits, plants and other medicinal things in this kingdom.)
Gregorio Losa Vila y Palomares, translated by Geogorio Loza-Balsa. La Paz: Sociedad Geográfica, 1983. 285p. bibliog.
A fascinating 18th-century inventory and guide to local medical practices.

570 **Development of a method for the concentration of rotaviruses from water and its application to field sampling.**
Gary A. Toranzos Soria. PhD dissertation, University of Arizona, Tucson, 1985. 176p. bibliog.
Since 1973, rotaviruses have been reported to be responsible for water-borne outbreaks of gastro-enteritis. The simian rotavirus (SAII) was used as a model for the human strains during the development of a method for concentrating

rotaviruses from drinking water. There were no reports of enteric viruses in water in Colombia or Bolivia. The results suggest a need to establish a virus-monitoring system.

571 **The distribution of hemoglobin in normal subjects at high altitude in Bolivia.**
J. D. Haas. *American Journal of Physical Anthropology*, vol. 63, no. 2 (1986).
Presents data to establish normal levels of haemoglobin for a population resident at an altitude of 3,600 metres in La Paz, Bolivia.

572 **The effect of high altitude on the growth of children of high socioeconomic status in Bolivia.**
S. Stinson. *American Journal of Physical Anthropology*, vol. 59, no. 1 (Sept. 1982), p. 61-71. bibliog.
Describes the physical growth of middle and upper-middle class children resident in La Paz. The sample consisted of 323 children between 8 and 14 years of age. Children who lived at high altitude all their lives were found to be smaller than those who did not.

573 **Enfermedad y salud según la concepción aymará-quechua.** (Sickness and health in the Amyará-Quechua mind.)
Federico Aguilo. Sucre: Qori Llama, 1982. 233p. bibliog.
A study of native concepts of health, fitness and illness.

574 **Fetal hypoxia at high-altitude: hematological comparisons from Bolivia.**
Claudette C. Ballew. *American Journal of Physical Anthropology*, vol. 63, no. 2 (1984), p. 136.
Concludes that the foetus at high altitude experiences a greater degree of hypoxic stress *in utero* than the foetus at low altitude. The degree of hypoxic stress is mediated by parity and ethnic group.

575 **Grass, roots, herbs, promotors and preventions. A reevaluation of contemporary international health care planning: the Bolivian case.**
L. Crandon. *Social Science and Medicine*, vol. 17, no. 17 (1983), p. 1,281-89.
Modern community-based medicine seeks to combine the traditional use of herbs and respect for local customs with the use of modern medicine. Such programmes can also be found in Guatemala.

576 **Health status of migrants.**
Betsy Foxman, Ralph R. Frerichs, James N. Becht. *Human Biology*, vol. 56, no. 1 (1984), p. 129-41.
Examines the health of migrants, including morbidity, mortality and fertility patterns.

577 **Human fertility and land tenure in highland Bolivia.**
Ricardo A. Godoy. *Social Biology*, vol. 31, nos 3-4 (1984), p. 290-97.
Compares demographic data for landless and landed peasants from northern Potosí. Household size and birth rates are larger and higher in the highland areas than in the valleys. Among highland people no significant difference was observed in the fertility of landed and landless women. Traditional exchange and reciprocity seems to negate differences in fertility, mortality and socio-economic status.

578 **Maximal aerobic power, nutritional status and activity level in Bolivia-Aparapitas.**
Lawrence P. Greska (et al.). *American Journal of Physical Anthropology*, vol. 57, no. 2 (1982), p. 194.
Maximal aerobic power has been shown to be related to productivity and to nutritional status in undernourished men. This suggests that productivity may be affected by nutrional status.

579 **Nutritional status of a group of Bolivians living in the state of Cochabamba.**
Effat Abdel-Kader Zahran. PhD dissertation, University of North Carolina at Greensboro, 1982. 181p. bibliog.
The nutritional status of 710 Bolivians was evaluated in connection with the USAID project for the promotion of soybean utilization. Rural and urban families in Cochabamba were included in the study and, of these, only six per cent followed diets which provided adequate nutrients and energy.

580 **Second external evaluation of the Bolivian Food for Development Program (PL480-Title III): its institutional performance and impact on farmers.**
John K. Hatch (et al.). New York: Rural Development Services, 1984. 136p.
Using eighteen peasant para-technicians as field researchers, the author examines the impact of the Food for Development Programme on Bolivians.

581  **Socioeconomic status and child growth in rural Bolivia.**
S. Stinson.  *Ecology of Food and Nutrition*, vol. 13, no. 3 (1983),
p. 179-87.
Use social and economic data to examine and explain why poorer rural children in
Bolivia are small in size.

582  **Variation in body-composition by altitude in Bolivian newborns.**
Claudette C. Ballew.  *American Journal of Physical
Anthropology*, vol. 66, no. 2 (1985), p. 167.
Compares the body composition of 174 highland newborn babies to 69 lowland
newborn babies. High-altitude babies were 350 grammes lighter and 1 cm shorter,
but had an additional 4.5 mm in skinfolds; differences were not linked to poor
nutrition.

583  **Work and caloric stress among Bolivian porters.**
T. L. Leatherman (et al.).  *American Journal of Physical
Anthropology*, vol. 60, no. 2 (1983), p. 218.
Studies how poor nutrition affects the ability of Aymará men to perform their
daily work as porters in La Paz.

# Languages

## General

584 **América latina, en sus lenguas indígenas.** (Latin America, and her indigenous languages.)
Edited by Bernard Pottier; United Nations Educational, Scientific and Cultural Organization (UNESCO). Caracas: Monte Avila Editores, C. A., 1983. 476p. maps. bibliog.

Part of the UNESCO series entitled 'América latina en su cultura'. Previous volumes dealt with music, literature, etc. Pottier brings together a collection of essays by noted linguists, including Xavier Albó, Victor Hugo Cardenas, Yolanda Lastra de Suarez, Bernard Pottier and Louisa R. Stark. The volume is organized into six parts: (1) an historical overview, and the politics of linguistics during the colonial era; (2) multilingualism; (3) native languages and the formation of dialects; (4) linguistic structures; (5) social linguistics; and (6) an extensive bibliography. Also includes graphs and illustrations.

585 **Bolivian Indian grammars.**
Ester Matteson. Norman, Oklahoma: University of Oklahoma Press, 1967. 2 vols.

Presents ten grammars of Bolivian Indian languages. Volume one contains Baure, Ignaciano, Tacana, Eseeja and Chacobo. Volume two includes Quechua, Guaraní, Sirionó, Itonama, Movima. The grammars were prepared by linguists fluent in the spoken languages, but these treatments were not exhaustive.

586  **Classification of South American Indian languages.**
Čestmír Loukokka.   Los Angeles: University of California, 1968.
4th ed. 453p. maps. bibliog.
An introduction to native South American languages and a good starting place for
a new student.

587  **The future of oppressed languages in the Andes.**
Xavier Albó.   In: *Peasants, primitives and proletariats: the struggle
for identity in South America.* Edited by David Browman, Ronald
Schwartz. New York: Mouton, 1979, p. 267-88.
Focuses on the role of Indian languages (Quechua and Aymará) as social
classifiers, and on how languages function to maintain group boundaries. This
essay also discusses 'double monolingualism' and how it is used to oppress those
who only speak indigenous languages. It also outlines the argument for the
extinction of Indian languages and presents an alternative view which favours
their survival.

588  **The languages of South American Indians.**
J. H. Steward.   In: *Handbook of South American Indians.*
Edited by Julian H. Steward. Washington, DC: US Government
Printing Office, vol.6 (1948), p. 157-318.
The *Handbook* is the best source of information on Indian culture and languages.

589  **South American Indian languages: retrospect and prospect.**
Harriet E. Manelis Klein, Louisa R. Stark.   Austin, Texas:
University of Texas Press, 1985. 863p. bibliog.
A book of readings by experts on languages and culture. Part two, entitled
'Indigenous languages of the Andes', deals with the Quechua and Aymará
languages. Essays include: Lucy T. Briggs' 'A critical survey of the literature on
the Aymará language' (p. 546-94); and 'Dialectical variation in Aymara' (p. 595-
616); M. J. Hardman's 'Aymará and Quechua language in contact' (p. 617-43)
and Bruce Mannhein's 'Contact and Quechua external genetic relationships'
(p. 644-90).

# Aymará

590  **The Aymará language in its social and cultural context: a collection
of essays on aspects of Aymará language and culture.**
M. J. Hardman.   Gainesville, Florida: University of Florida Press,
1981. 317p. bibliog. (University of Florida Social Science Monograph, no. 67).
A collection of twenty-two essays on the Aymará language. Subjects covered

include: Aymará grammatical and semantic categories; the Aymará language in contact with other languages; and the implications of Aymará studies for applied anthropological linguistics.

591 **Aymará syntactic relations and derivational verb suffixes.**
Eusebia Herimia Martin. *Anthropological Linguistics*, vol. 44, no. 2 (1978), p. 131–36.
Describes the reflexive, human causative, beneficiary and prejudical suffixes of Aymará verbs in combination with substantive suffixes which indicate a complementary relationship between the substantive and the verb.

592 **Compendio de la gramatíca kechua y aymará; seguido de un vocabulario completo.** (Textbook of Quechua and Aymará grammar; followed by a complete vocabulary.)
Germán G. Villamor. La Paz: Librería Popular, 1942. 157p.
A dated but still useful textbook, suitable for beginners.

593 **De adaneva a Inkarrí; una visión indígena del Perú.** (An indigenous vision of Peru.)
Alejandro Ortiz Rescaniere. Lima: Retablo de Papel, 1973. 189p. bibliog.
Quechua and Aymará selections with Spanish translations. Studies Andean myths with original texts and postulates that the Peruvian cosmology is a defence against society. The material in this work has a strong messianic element.

594 **Enseñanza del idioma aymará como segundo idioma.** (Aymará as a second language.)
Juan de Dios Yapita. La Paz: Instituto de la Lengua y Cultura Aymará, 1981. 292p. bibliog.
Discusses the introduction and development of programmes to teach Aymará as a second language. They represent part of a national effort to produce a bilingual culture in Bolivia.

595 **Fábulas orales aymaras: año de la mujer peruana.** (Aymará folktales: year of the Peruvian woman.)
Mario Franco Inojosa. Juli, Peru: [n.p.]. 1975. 190p.
A selection of peasant folk-tales, translated into Spanish. These tales were used by parents, particularly mothers, to educate and socialize their children. Such tales have great anthropological value. This work contains some fifty tales, about half of which focus on the fox as a central character.

596 **Gramática y diccionario aimara.** (Aymará grammar and dictionary.)
Juan Enrique Ebbing. La Paz: Editorial y Librería Don Bosco, 1965. 360p.

In addition to the grammar, there is a pronunciation guide, an Aymará–Spanish, Spanish–Aymará dictionary, an index and a verb table.

597 **Lecciones de aimará: premier y segunda niveles.** (Aymará lessons: first and second levels.)
Joaquín Herrero. Cochabamba, Bolivia: Instituto de Idiomas Padres de Maryknoll, 2 vols. 1969, 1972.

Two volumes of Aymará language lessons. This study follows the ALM method of repetition and substitution drills, dialogues, and translation exercises. A vocabulary and an index are also included.

598 **La lengua de Adan y el hombre de Tiaguanaco. Resumen de estas obras.** (The language of Adam and the Man of Tiahuanaco: a summary of these works.)
Emeterio Villamil de Rada. La Paz: Imprenta Artistica, 1939. 235p.

A classic and controversial study of the origins of the Aymará language. Villamil de Rada maintained that Aymará was the original language of Adam, or of mankind.

599 **Manual practico ABC del aymará, quechua, y castellana.** (Practical ABC manual of Aymará, Quechua, and Spanish.)
Lima: Ediciones Tiempos Modernos, 1975. 112p.

A modern textbook containing phrases and common expressions in three languages. They are listed under various headings, such as greetings, family, travel, food, etc.

600 **Moderno vocabulario del quechua y del aymará y su correspondencia en castellano.** (Modern Quechua and Aymará vocabulary with a corresponding Spanish section.)
Germán Villamor. La Paz: Editorial Popular, 1981. 4th ed. 168p.

A standard tool in language teaching in Bolivia.

601 **Supuesta derivación summero-asiria de las lenguas kechua y aymará.** (On the supposed Syrian-Assyrian origins of the Quechua and Aymará languages.)
Samuel A. LaFone y Quevedo. Buenos Aires: Conti hermanos, 1901. 11p. bibliog.

Argues that Andean languages developed originally from ancient middle eastern cultures.

602 **Vocabulario de la lengua aymará.** (Vocabulary of the Aymará language.)
Ludovico Bertonio. Cochabamba, Bolivia: Centro de Estudios de la Realidad Económica y Social, 1984. 474p.
A new edition of a vocabulary book which was originally published in 1612.

# Guaraní

603 **Ayvu Rapyta: textos míticos de los Mybá-Guaraní del Guairá.** (The basis of human language: mythical texts of the Mybá-Guaraní Indians of the Guairá.)
Edited by Leon Cadagan. São Paulo: Universidade de São Paulo, Faculdade de Filosofia, Ciencias e Letra, 1959. 217p. (Boletim no. 227, Antropología, no. 5).
Presents myths and legends in Guaraní and Spanish. A vocabulary is also included.

604 **A description of coloquial Guaraní.**
Emma Gregores, Jorge A. Suárez. Paris: Mouton, 1967. 248p.
Gives information on the linguistic classification of Guaraní and reviews the literature and written sources which are available. The text includes grammar, phonology and morphemics.

605 **Diccionario castellano–guaraní y guaraní–castellano: sintáctico, fraseológico, ideológico.** (Spanish–Guarani, Guarani–Spanish dictionary; syntax, phraseology and ideology.)
Antonio Guasch. Asunción: Ediciones Loyola, 1980. 4th ed. 789p.
A basic Guaraní–Spanish dictionary and grammar text.

606 **El guaraní en la geografía de América.** (Guaraní in American geography.)
Anselmo Jover Peralta. Buenos Aires: Ediciones Tupa, 1950. 272p.
A basic study of the geographical distribution of the Guaraní language.

129

607 **Hispanismos en el guaraní: estudio sobre la penetración de la
cultura española en la guaraní, según se refleja en la lengua.**
(Hispanicism in Guaraní, a study of the penetration of Spanish
culture into Guaraní as reflected in the language.)
Marcos A. Morínigo.   Buenos Aires: Telleres Casa Jacabo
Peuser, 1931. 432p. maps. (Colección de estudios indigenistas, 1).
A short linguistic analysis accompanied by maps and diagrams. It also includes a
vocabulary section which is arranged by subject headings.

608 **Resumen de prehistoria y protohistoria de los paises guaranís;
conferencias dades en el colegio nacional de segunda ensenanza de la
Asunción dos dias de julio, 8 y 21 de agosto de 1913.** (Summary of
the prehistory and proto-history of the Guaraní countries; a
conference given in the national secondary school of Asunción on
two days in July, the 8 and 21 of August, 1913.)
Moisés Santiago Bertoni.   Asunción: J. E. O'Leary, 1914. 64p.
A study of the evolution of Guaraní culture and language.

# Quechua

609 **Ayacucho Quechua grammar and dictionary.**
Gary John Parker.   The Hague: Mouton, 1969. 221p. map.
bibliog.
A grammar and dictionary of the Ayacucho dialect of Quechua. It includes a
sample text with translations.

610 **Breve diccionario kechwa–español.** (Brief Quechua–Spanish
dictionary.)
Jorge A. Lira.   Cuzco: n.p. [n.d.]. 452p.
A Quechua–Spanish dictionary.

611 **Diccionario normalizado y comparativo quechua: Chachapoyas–
Lamas.** (Standard and comparative Quechuan dictionary:
Chachapoyas–Lamas dialect.)
Gerald Taylor.   Paris: L'Harmattan, 1979. 248p. (Série
ethnolinguistique amérindienne).
A dictionary of regional Quechua.

612 **Diccionario quechua.** (Quechua dictionary.)
Marinell Park. Lima: Ministerio de Educación, 1976. 188p.
Companion dictionary to the San Martin dialect grammar textbook.

613 **Diccionario quechua, Ancash–Huailis.** (Quechua dictionary,
Ancash–Huailis dialect.)
Gary John Parker, Amancio Chávez. Lima: Ministerio de
Educación, 1976. 311p.
This Spanish–Quechua dictionary also includes regional notations.

614 **Diccionario trí-lingüe: Quechua of Cusco, English, Spanish.**
Esteban Hornberger S. Lima: LCA, 1977, 3 vols.
A Quechua–Spanish–English dictionary.

615 **Elementos de gramática incana o quechua.** (Elements of Inca or
Quechua grammar.)
José Antonio Núñez del Prado. Cuzco: Garcilaso, 1960. 162p.
An elementary Quechua grammar textbook.

616 **La escritura del quechua: problemática y perspectivas.** (Writing
Quechua: problems and perspectives.)
Federico Aguiló. La Paz: Editorial los Amigos del Libro, 1987.
174p. bibliog.
Discusses the problems associated with writing Quechua, a language which
developed in an exclusively oral tradition.

617 **Expansión del quechua: primeros contactos con el castellano.**
(Expansion of Quechua: first contacts with the Spanish.)
Ibico Rojas R. Lima: Ediciones Signo, 1980. 131p. bibliog.
Discusses how the Quechua language spread after the arrival of the Spaniards,
who communicated with the native populations in their own language.

618 **Gramática kechwa.** (Quechua grammar.)
Cesar Augusto Guardia Mayorga. Lima: Ediciones los Andes,
1973. 388p.
A basic Quechua grammar textbook.

619 **Gramática quechua.** (Quechua grammar.)
David Coombs. Lima: Ministerio de Educacíon, 1976. 222p.
bibliog.
One of a series of six grammar textbooks prepared by the Peruvian Ministry of
Education. Each grammar has a companion dictionary. Each pair of books covers
a different Quechua dialect.

620 **Gramática quechua: enciclopedia de gramática quechua integral.**
(Quechua grammar: encyclopaedia of Quechua grammar.)
Braulio Garjeda Challco. Lima: Ediciones Instituto Superior de
Quechua de Peru, 1976. 273p.
A basic Quechua grammar textbook.

621 **An introduction to spoken Bolivian Quechua.**
Garland D. Bills, Bernardo Vallejo C., Rudolphe C. Troike.
Austin, Texas: University of Texas Press, 1969. 449p. map.
bibliog.
This text includes conversations, vocabulary, review drills, reading and visual aids
to help memorize dialogues. Companion tapes are also available.

622 **Literatura pre-hispánica y colonial.** (Prehispanic and colonial
literature.)
Edgar Avila Echazú. La Paz: Librería y Editorial Gisbert, 1974.
202p. bibliog.
Includes selections from the indigenous literature of the Inca and Spanish colonial
periods originally written in Quechua, but translated into Spanish.

623 **Metodo audio-oral para la ensenanza y el aprendizaje del idioma
quechua; gramática quechua.** (Audio-oral method for teaching and
learning the Quechua language; Quechua grammar.)
Daniel Bedriñana García. Lima: Editorial Inkari, 1975. 94p.
A Quechua language textbook which uses the audio-oral method of language
instruction.

624 **Los mil rostros del quechua: sociolingüística de Cochambamba.**
(The thousand faces of Quechua: a social linguistic study of
Cochambamba.)
Xavier Albó. Lima: Instituto de Estudios Peruanos, 1974. 268p.
(Serie Lengua y Sociedad, 1).
An anthropological study of language distribution and usage in central Bolivia.

625 **Poesía dramática de los Incas.** (Dramatic poetry of the Incas.)
Clements Robert Markham. Buenos Aires: C. Casavalle, 1883.
86p.
A collection of Inca poetry, compiled by a famous traveller and geographer.

626 **A Quechua legend of Peru – *Yaku Runa* or *'River Man.'***
Douglas W. Howkins. Glasgow: University of Glasgow, Institute
of Latin-American Studies, 1973. 211p. maps.
A translation of an Andean folk tale.

Languages. Quechua

627 **Quechua y aymará lenguas en contacto.** (Quechua and Aymará
languages in contact.)
Martha J. Hardman.   La Paz: *Antropología*, vol. 1 (1979),
p. 69-84.
Argues that Quechua enjoys a certain prestige as a language in Andean society
because it was originally the language of conquerors.

628 **El quechua y la historia social andina.** (Quechua and Andean social
history.)
Alfredo Torero.   Lima: Universidad Ricardo Palma, Dirreción
Universitaria de Investigación, 1974. 240p. map.
An examination and socio-historical evaluation of the Quechua language in the
greater Andean region.

# Religion

629 **At the crossroads of the earth and the sky: an Andean cosmology.**
Gary Dwayne Urton. Austin, Texas. University of Texas Press,
1981. 248p. maps.

This study of native religious beliefs presents much information on Inca and
Quechua cosmology. For example, the author discusses the constellations
representing the serpent, toad, llama and fox, and the cross which, to the native,
represents an axis along which a state of equilibrium is established and
maintained.

630 **Bolivia as a field of missionary endeavor.**
Catherine Cottingham. MA thesis, San Francisco Theological
Seminary, San Anselmo, California.

Examines the extent of missionary activity in Bolivia.

631 **Christianismo y religión quechua en la prelatura de Ayairril.**
(Christianity and Quechua religion in the prelature of Ayaivilli.)
Tomas Gair. Cusco, Bolivia: Instituto Pastoral Andina, 1972.
257p. bibliog.

An examination of the syncretic religious beliefs of highland populations.

632 **Christianismo y revolución en América latina.** (Christianity and
revolution in Latin America.)
Manuel M. Martínez. *Diogenes*, (summer 1974). 146p.

Examines the relationship between the Church and the revolutionary movements
in South America. This work also provides a good introduction to 'Liberation
Theology' and changes in the Roman Catholic Church.

633 **Church and education in a peripheral conflicting society of the contemporary world system. (A case-study of the Bolivian Catholic Bishops' Committee for Education (1970-1980).)**
Eduardo González-Saa. PhD dissertation, Stanford University, Stanford, California, 1984. 357p. bibliog.
Examines the influence of the Bolivian Catholic Church on national education during the period 1970 to 1980, with emphasis on the Bishops' Education Committee, whose central commitment has been to make education in Bolivia more democratic.

634 **Church and state in Latin America: a history of politico ecclesiastical relations.**
J. Lloyd Mecham. Chapel Hill, North Carolina: University of North Carolina Press, 1934. 550p. bibliog.
The best available survey of Church-state relations after Independence. A section on Bolivia is included (p. 221-46).

635 **Church growth in the high Andes.**
Keith D. Hamilton. Lucknow, India: Institute of Church Growth, 1962. 146p.
A study of the growth and success of the evangelical movement in Bolivia, Peru and Ecuador.

636 **The Church in Bolivia.**
Translated by John Drury. In: *Between honesty and hope.* New York: Maryknoll Publications, 1970, p. 140-47.
Bolivian priests urge their bishops to join with them and make the Roman Catholic Church in Bolivia a church dedicated to helping the poor.

637 **Commandos for Christ.**
Bruce Porterfield. New York: Harper, 1963. 238p.
Tales of modern missionary activity of the New Tribes Mission among Bolivia's Indian populations.

638 **The condor of the jungle, pioneer pilot of the Andes.**
C. Peter Wagner, Joseph S. McCollough. Westwood, California: Revell, 1966. 158p.
A biography of Wally Hernon of the Andes Evangelical Mission. Hernon was one of the first Protestant missionaries to be successful in the evangelical effort in early 20th-century Bolivia.

639 **Distribution of the *mesa* in Latin America.**
Douglas Sharon. *Journal of Latin America Lore*, vol. 2, no. 1
(summer 1976), p. 71-95. bibliog.

Studies the use of a *mesa* (table or altar) arrangement of power objects used by
shamans in Mesoamerica and the Andean regions of South America. Also
contains a good bibliography on native religions and folk medicine and healing.

640 **From football field to mission field with Richard Hayden.**
Gwendolen Hayden. Washington, DC: Review & Herald, 1951.
318p.

A personal history of the life of a missionary's wife in the Bolivian Amazon and
the Lake Titicaca regions.

641 **From the Sun of the Incas to the Virgin of Copacabana.**
Sabine G. MacCormack. *Representations*, vol. 8 (1984), p. 30-60.

Examines Inca and Christian pilgrimages to the sacred site of the Temple of the
Sun and the Virgin of Copacabana, Bolivia.

642 **God planted five seeds.**
Jean Dye Johnson. New York: Harper, 1966. 213p.

A history of missionaries who were killed by the Ayare Indians of Bolivia in 1943.
The missionaries were members of the New Tribes Mission.

643 **In and out of the Andes.**
Sister María del Rey (Maryknoll). New York: Charles Scribner's,
1954. 281p.

A chatty, personal memoir of a Maryknoll nun's mission tour in Bolivia.

644 **Lightning in the folklife and religion of the central Andes.**
Daniel W. Gade. *Anthropos*, vol. 78, nos 5-6 (1983), p. 770-88.

Discusses the influences of lightning on native religious beliefs and Christianity.

645 **Missionary moments.**
Phyllis Cammack. Newberg, Oregon: Barclay Press, 1966. 134p.

An interesting and well-written history of 13 years spent working as a missionary
with Bolivia's Aymará Indians.

646 **Missionary pioneering in Bolivia, with some account of work in
Argentina.**
Will Payne, Charles T. W. Wilson. London: H. A. Raymond,
[1901]. 148p. maps.

Designed to give Christian workers an intelligent outline of the existing state of
missionary activity in Latin America, this work also names many of the early
missionaries who worked in the region.

647 **Protestant Christianity in Bolivia: mission theory and practice in three mission churches.**

Wilson Texter Boots.   PhD dissertation, American University, Washington, DC, 1971. 325p. bibliog.

Examines and discusses the relative success of various Protestant missions in converting Bolivians to Protestantism.

648 **Protestant missionary activity and freedom of religion in Ecuador, Peru, and Bolivia.**

Paul E. Kuhl.   PhD dissertation, Southern Illinois University, Carbondale, Illinois, 1983. 508p.

Examines the role of Protestant missionary activity in securing freedom of religion rights. Missionary activity played a major role in persuading the Peruvians to liberalize their laws but was only of minor significance in Bolivia and Ecuador.

649 **The Protestant movement in Bolivia.**

C. Peter Wagner.   South Pasadena, California: William Carey Library, 1970. 240p. maps. bibliog.

A comprehensive study of the evolution and present vitality of Protestantism in Bolivia and the various organizations working most effectively there. This is an excellent source on active Protestant churches and missions which contains a wealth of information on the subject.

650 **Protestantism in Bolivia.**

David Phillips.   Unpublished MA thesis, University of Calgary, Canada, 1968.

An overview of Protestantism in Bolivia up to 1952, written by a Canadian Baptist missionary.

651 **Ripening fruit: a history of the Bolivian Indian mission.**

Margarita Allen Hudspith.   Harrington Park, New Jersey: Harrington Press, 1958. 158p.

A history of the Andes Evangelical Mission, an early and reasonably successful Protestant missionary effort.

652 **Theological education in Latin America.**

C. Peter Wagner.   *Christianity Today* (15 March 1963), p. 21-22.

A short, general survey from a conservative point of view.

653 **Today's missions in the Latin American social revolution.**

C. Peter Wagner.   *Evangelical Missions Quarterly*, vol. 1, no. 2 (1965), p. 19-29.

Examines the difficult role of the foreign missionary in the revolutionary process. Wagner poses the question: does the missionary become involved in this type of political liberation movement, or does he continue to tend parochial matters?

# Education

## General

654 **Counselor training in Bolivia – problems and possibilities.**
A. D. Heinzen. *Personnel and Guidance Journal*, vol. 61, no. 8 (1983), p. 501-04.

Describes and examines how guidance counsellors are trained in Bolivia, where 1,400 classroom hours are needed to qualify for professional standing. The training programme suffers from a lack of appropriate materials and teachers because of a general lack of resources.

655 **Creación de la pedagogía nacional.** (The creation of a national pedagogy.)
Franz Tamayo. La Paz: Biblioteca del Sesquicentenario de la República, 1975. 226p.

A collection of fifty-five articles which focus on the need to develop an educational system free from external influences.

656 **Cultural policy in Bolivia.**
Mariano Baptista Gumucio. Paris: United Nations Educational, Scientific and Cultural Organization (UNESCO), 1978. 81p.

Discusses Bolivian eductional goals, policy and institutions in the broader context of a national cultural policy.

657 **Desarrollo y universidad.** (Development and the university.)
Ricardo Anaya. La Paz: Librería y Editorial 'Juventud', 1975.
206p. bibliog.
A collection of essays which discuss the university in Bolivia in the context of
national social, economic and political issues. Anaya was a leader of the 1919
University Reform Movement at the University of Cochabamba.

658 **Educación, familia, y participación económica femenina en la
Argentina.** (Education, family and female economic participation
in Argentina).
Catalina H. Wainerman. *Desarrollo Económico*, vol. 18, no. 72
(Jan.-March 1979), p. 511-37. bibliog.
Part of a research project by the Centro de Estudios de Población entitled
'Participation of women in the economic activity of Argentina, Bolivia and
Paraguay'. This study examines how family life is altered by the fact that women
now work in non-traditional areas.

659 **The effect of primary-school quality on academic achievement
across twenty-nine high- and low-income countries.**
Stephen P. Heyneman, William A. Loxley. *American Journal of
Sociology*, vol. 88, no. 6 (May 1983), p. 1,162-94.
Children who attend primary school in low-income countries like Bolivia learn
less than those in developed ones. The lower the income of the country, the lower
the educational performance and a child's social status becomes less of a variable.
The authors conclude that the predominant influence on learning is the quality of
the schools and teachers.

660 **Estudio de la educación rural boliviana: historia organización,
función y recursos.** (A study of rural Bolivian education: history,
organization, function and resources.)
Marcelo Sangines Uriarte. La Paz: CIDA, 1967. 141p. bibliog.
A very fine study of the rural education programme implemented after the 1952
revolution. Education is seen as playing a vital role in the integration of the rural
classes into national life.

661 **Interpersonal influences on education aspirations: cross-cultural
analysis.**
William Spencer. *Sociology of Education*, vol. 49, no. 1 (1976),
p. 41-46.
Studies the education aspirations of seventh grade students in Bolivia. This essay
was based on an American model and concludes that interpersonal influences
mediate the effects of structural variables on educational aspirations. However,
more comparative studies are needed, in order to test the universality of this.

662 **Mito y realidad de la educación boliviano.** (Myth and reality in Bolivian education.)

Eduardo Cortes León.   Cochabamba, Bolivia: Editorial 'Serrano', 1973. 227p. bibliog.

Discusses the failure of the government to implement the 1955 educational codes in Bolivia, particularly in the rural zones. As a result, educational opportunities of the most basic sort are still lacking in Bolivia. Illiteracy is an obstacle to national integration and economic development, and effectively marginalizes the majority of the population.

663 **Research notes: social selectivity in the secondary schools of Buenos Aires, La Paz and Santiago de Chile.**

Robert Myers, Edward Clearly, Joseph Fischer, Michael Petty. *Sociology of Education*, vol. 43, no. 3 (1973), p. 355-60.

Studies how students and their families select the school they will attend. The patterns of selectivity and the types of school that are available vary in the three cities. The elimination of private schools does not eliminate social selectivity because distinctions are also made between schools in the public sector.

664 **Los sistemas educativos de los paises signatarios del Convenio Andres Bello.** (The educational systems of the signatory countries of the Andres Bello Convention.)

Bogota, Colombia: Ministerio del Educación Nacional, 1974. 287p.

Gives detailed descriptions of the educational systems of Bolivia, Colombia, Ecuador, Peru and Venezuela based on data supplied by government agencies and world organizations.

665 **The structure of educational costs: multiproduct cost functions for primary and secondary schools in Latin America.**

Emmanuel Jimenez.   *Economics of Education Review*, vol. 5, no. 11 (1986), p. 25-39.

Data for Bolivia and Paraguay suggest that economies of scale do operate in the running of an average primary school. This paper expands the literature on educational cost functions and uses data from Bolivian and Paraguayan case-studies.

666 **Visión cuantitativa de la educación privada en Bolivia.** (A quantitative vision of private education in Bolivia.)

La Paz: Comisión Episcopal de Educación, 1976.

A wide-ranging study of the 1970-74 period, based on data collected from a questionnaire. No analysis of the data is presented.

# Bilingualism

667 **Bilingual education in Bolivia.**
Lucy T. Briggs. In: *Bilingualism: social issues and policy implications*. Edited by Andrew W. Miracle. Athens: University of Georgia Press, 1983, p. 84-95. 188p.

Briggs, a respected Aymará scholar, reviews Bolivian educational policy which has as one of its objectives the universal teaching of the Spanish language, but which neglects native languages as a result. She argues that a few modest programmes should be introduced to teach local idioms, and for the future, suggests that the government should train large numbers of teachers in bilingual techniques.

668 **Castellanizer al pueblo aymará.** (To Hispanize the Aymará people.)
Manuel F. de Lucca D. *Temas Sociales* (June 1971), p. 108-12.

Describes the unsuccessful efforts to teach the Spanish language to the Aymará-speaking Indians of Bolivia, and to oversee the creation of a bilingual rural population.

669 **Idiomas, escuelas y radios en Bolivia.** (Languages, schools and radios in Bolivia.)
Xavier Albó. Lima: Centro de Investigación Lingüística Alplicada, Universidad Nacional Mayor de San Marcos, 1977. 55p. bibliog.

Deals with radio broadcasts in the native languages of the Aymará and Quechua. These programmes are often overwhelmed by Spanish culture, especially in the schools.

670 **The mutual influences of Spanish and Andean languages.**
M. J. Hardman de Bautista. *Word*, vol. 33, nos 1-2 (1982), p. 143-57.

Language interaction in the Andes has resulted in changes in grammar, and the Spanish spoken in the region reflects the contributions of indigenous tongues. This article deals with phonology and lexicography in a cultural and historical context and concludes that Spanish, together with Aymará influences, codifies and reflects the Andean reality.

671 **Quechua/Spanish bilingual education and language policy in Bolivia (1977-1982).**
Donald H. Burns. *International Education Journal*, vol. 2, 1984, p. 197-220.

Explains and examines the many problems associated with extending bilingual education throughout Bolivia. A principal impediment was the preference among educators for imposing Spanish on peasants in the name of 'national unity'.

# Films and the Film Industry

## Documentary

672 **Andean women.**
Faces of Change Series. American Universities Field Staff, 1974.
18 mins., sound, subtitles, colour. Available through Indiana
University Audio Visual Center. Catalog number GSC-1390.

An excellent film which shows the position of Aymará women who perform many tasks vital to society and yet who see themselves only as helpers. It also explores the cultural ideal of society. See also William W. Johnson's *The Andean republics: Bolivia, Chile, Ecuador, Peru* (q.v.), and his *Bolivia: an undiscovered land* (q.v.).

673 **Blood of the condor.**
Directed by Jorge Sanjines. 72 mins. Quechua and Spanish
dialogue with English subtitles, black-and-white. Available through
Unifilm, New York City. Cable: UNIFILM NEW YORK.

Offers a fascinating anthropological look at the life-style of the Quechua Indians. Also, it dramatically demonstrates the relationship of the Indian communities to the rest of Bolivian society, especially mestizo society.

674 **The children know.**
Faces of Change Series. American University Field Staff, 1974.
33 mins., sound, subtitles colour. Available through Indiana
University Audio Visual Center. Catalog number GSC-1388.

Explores the deep division in Andean society between *campesinos* and mestizos. Prejudices are seen through the eyes of children. The film illustrates that these begin at birth, are perpetuated by the schools and continue throughout life.

142

675 **Chuquiago.**
Directed by Antonio Eguino.   87 mins., Aymará and Spanish
dialogue with English subtitles, colour. Available through Unifilm,
New York City. Cable: UNIFILM NEW YORK.

Chuquiago is the native name for La Paz. In four separate, yet overlapping,
stories, Chuquiago examines the lives of individuals from four different social
settings. The characters include an Indian boy hired out to work by his parents,
an Indian teenager who wants to assimilate into white culture, a government
bureaucrat and, Patricia, a university student.

676 **Magic and Catholicism.**
Faces of Change Series. American University Field Staff, 1974.
33 mins., sound and colour, English subtitles. Avalable through
Indian University Audio Visual Center. Catalog number
GCS-1392.

Examines religious syncretism in Vitocota. Syncretic religion characteristically
combines elements from two, or more, different perspectives to make a
comfortable, tension-free relationship. While a Western viewer observes peasants
celebrating a Catholic fiesta and a traditional ceremony for insuring a good
harvest, the *campesinos* perceive the same events as being part of a total and
coherent system.

677 **Potato planters.**
Faces of Change Series. American University Field Staff, 1974.
17 mins., sound, subtitles, colour. Available through Indiana
University Audio Visual Center. Catalog number GSC-1389.

Compares the daily life of an Aymará family, which is simple and routine, with
the complexity of their belief system. It also studies agriculture in the village of
Vitocota, the land tenure system, crops and diet, and sex roles. See also *The
Andean republics: Bolivia, Chile, Ecuador, Peru* (q.v.) and *Bolivia: an
undiscovered land* (q.v.).

678 **The spirit possession of Alejandro Mamani.**
Faces of Change Series. American University Field Staff, 1974.
28 mins., sound and colour, English subtitles. Available through
Indiana University Audio Visual Center. Catalog number GCS-
1391.

This film portrays an old man, with property and status, who is nearing the end of
his life, but lacks contentment. He believes he is possessed by evil spirits.

679 **Viacocha: the Aymará of the Bolivian Andes.**
Faces of Change Series. American University Field Staff, 1974.
30 mins., sound subtitles, colour. Available through Indiana
University Audio Visual Center. Catalog number GSC-1387.

Mestizos and *campesinos* in the Andean highlands intereact within a new subsistence economic system. This documentary examines market days and fiestas as times of interaction between the two groups. Mestizos exhibit alternately benign and abusive behaviour to assert their traditional social dominance over the peasantry.

# Criticism

680 **The Aymará of the Bolivian Andes: a review of six films.**
Murdo J. MacLeod. *Latin American Research Review*, vol. 11, no. 1 (1976), p. 228-32.

A review of six excellent films made by the American University Field Staff in the Bolivian highland regions among the Aymará-speaking peasantry.

681 **Cine boliviano 1953-1983: aproximación a una experiencia.**
(Bolivian cinema, 1953-1983: approaching reality.)
Carlos D. Mesa Gisbert. In: *Tendencias actuales en la literatura boliviana.* (Present trends in Bolivian literature.) Edited by Jorge Sanjines. Minneapolis, Kansas: Institute for the Study of Ideologies and Literature; Instituto de Cine, Radio y Televisión, 1985. 284p.

An excellent introductory study of the Bolivian film industry. For a discussion of the period before 1953, see *Historia del cine boliviana* (A history of the Bolivian cinema) by Alfonso Gumucio Dagron (Mexico City: Filmoteca UNAM, 1983. 327p.) The author discusses Luis Castilo González, and provides a comprehensive list of all films and film-makers from 1904 onwards.

682 **Chuquiago: convergence and divergence in Bolivia's social caste.**
Willy Oscar Muñoz. In: *National traditions in motion pictures.* Edited by Douglas Radcliff-Umstead. Kent, Ohio: Romance Languages Department, Kent State University, 1985, p. 32-36. 106p.

Examines social realism and the study of class relations in the Bolivian cinema.

683 **Film as a revolutionary weapon: a Jorge Sanjines retrospective.**
Leon Campbell, Carlos Cortes. *History Teacher*, vol. 12, no. 3 (1979), p. 383-402.

Discusses five full-length films by the Bolivian director, Jorge Sanjines, who used film to document the peasants' revolutionary activity in Bolivia. His films are used to develop mass consciousness and to bring about a better understanding of popular culture in Bolivia. His first films are more radical than the later ones, but in total they make a powerful statement about national culture and the plight of the masses in Bolivia. The Bolivian film industry generally produces high quality products. This is an excellent introduction to this neglected area.

684  **A filmmaker's journal**
   Hubert Smith.   Hanover, New Hampshire: American Universities Field Staff. 1976. 25p. (West Coast South America Series, vol. 23, no. 2).
Describes personal reactions to, and professional methods for, making ethnographical films in Bolivia among the Aymará Indians. A total of six films were made.

685  **Jorge Sanjines ou comment créer un cinéma andin.** (Jorge Sanjines and the emergence of Andean film making.)
   Olivia Harris.   *Cahiers du Monde Hispanique et Luso-Brésilien*, vol. 44 (1985), p. 33-37.
Examines the career of Bolivia's leading film-maker. See also *Historia del cine boliviana* (q.v.) for biographical data on Jorge Sanjines and Jorge Ruiz.

686  **Neo-realism in contemporary Bolivian cinema: a case study of Jorge Sanjine's 'Blood of the Condor' and Antonio Eguino's 'Chuquiago'.**
   Jose H. Sanchez.   PhD dissertation, University of Michigan, Ann Arbor, 1983. 325p.
Studies the cinematic approaches of two contemporary Bolivian filmmakers, Jorge Sanjines and Antonio Eguino, and contends that Sanjine's film 'Blood of the condor' was mislabelled 'militant' cinema and that it is neo-realist, and that Eguino's 'Chuquiago' is neo-realistic in a limited sense.

# Literature

## General

**687** **Las cien obras capitales de la literatura boliviana.** (One hundred major works of Bolivian literature.)
Juan Siles Guevara.   La Paz: Editorial los Amigos del Libro, 1975. 513p. bibliog. (Enciclopedia Boliviana).

Discusses one hundred of the best examples of Bolivian writing. The volume is arranged by author, but includes the following topics; the short story, journalism, biography, the essay, history, poetry and the theatre.

**688** **Esquema de literatura virreinal en Bolivia.** (Scheme of viceregal literature in Bolivia.)
Teresa Gisbert.   La Paz: Dirección Nacional de Informaciones, 1963. 49p.

Examines 17th and 18th-century writers and includes chapters on Indian theatre, poetry, religious chronologies, the study of languages, socio-economic studies, and histories and travellers' accounts.

**689** **Estudios de literatura bolivianos.** (Studies in Bolivian literature.)
Gabriel Rene-Moreno.   La Paz: Biblioteca de Sesquicentenario de la República, 1975. 290p. bibliog.

A new edition of a classic study of Bolivian literature written by the doyen of Bolivian literature and history, Rene-Moreno. It includes the first of his biographies of national writers and his attempts at literary criticism. Entries presented here frequently appeared initially in Chilean reviews in the 19th and 20th centuries. Subjects covered include: *poetas bolivianos*, Manuel José Tovar, María Josefa Mujía, Mariano Ramollo, Néstor Gallindo, Ricardo J. Bustamante and Daniel Calvo.

690 **Letras bolivianas de hoy: Renato Prada y Pedro Shimose.** (Bolivian
writers of today: Renato Prada and Pedro Shimose.)
José Ortega. Buenos Aires: Fernando García Cambeiro, 1973.
115p. bibliog. (Colección Estudins Latinoamericanos, 5).

Following a good, brief historical introduction to Bolivian national literature, two
important younger Bolivian writers are presented; Prada, a writer of short stories,
and Shimose, a poet. An excellent bibliography is included.

691 **Narrativa hispanoamericana, 1816-1981: historia y antologia.**
(Hispanic-American narrative 1816-1981: history and anthology.)
Edited by Angel Flores, introduction by Antonio Skámeta.
Mexico City: Siglo XXI, 1985, 2 vols.

An anthology of modern Peruvian, Chilean and Bolivian literature. Volume four
entitled 'La generación de 1940-1969' (532p.), gives a general overview of Latin-
American authors of that period. Volume seven, entitled 'La generación de 1939
en adelante: Bolivia, Chile, Peru' (414p.), deals specifically with the South
Andes. Bolivian authors included are: Pedro Shimose Kawamura, Jaime
Nistahua, Raul Teixido, Felix Salazar González, Ramon Rocha Monroy, Rene
Bascopé Aspiazu and Manuel Vargas. Valuable bio-bibliographical data are
presented on each author.

692 **Prosa y verso de Bolivia.** (Prose and verse of Bolivia.)
Porfirio Díaz Machicao. La Paz: Editorial los Amigos del Libro,
1969. 4 vols. (Enciclopedia Boliviana).

A comprehensive guide to major Bolivian writers of the national period,
regardless of their writing discipline and their school of literature.

693 **Tendencias actuales en la literatura boliviana.** (Present trends in
Bolivian literature.)
Edited by Jorge Sanjines. Minneapolis, Minnesota: Institute for
the Study of Ideologies and Literature; Instituto de Cine, Radio y
Televisión, 1985. 284p.

A book of mainly bibliographical and review essays concerning the status of
contemporary literature in Bolivia. Includes: (1) Leonardo García Pabon's
'Aproximación a la critica literaria en Bolivia 1960-1980'; (2) Wilma Á. Torrico's
'Indice bibliográfico de libros de crítica y ensay literario bolivianos publicade
entre 1960-1980'; and (3) 'Indice bibliográfico de libros de poesía bolivianos,
1960-1980'; (4) Luis J. Antezana's 'La novela boliviana en el último cuarto de
siglo'; (5) Carlos Mesa Gisbert's 'Bibliográfica de la novela boliviana (1962-
1980)'; (6) Ruben Vargas Portugal's 'Indice bibliográfico de libros de poesía
bolivianos, 1960-1980'; (7) Ana Rebeca Prada's 'El cuento contemporáneo de la
represión en Bolivia'; and (8) Ocascar Munoz C., 'El teatro nacional en busca de
un punto de partida: 1967'.

# Criticism

694 **Arguedas: *Raza de Bronce*. (Arguedas: *Race of Bronze*.)**
Rodolfo A. Borello. *Cuadernos Hispanoamericanos*, vol. 417
(March 1985), p. 112-27. bibliog.
Examines the *pueblo enfermo* theme in Bolivian literature.

695 **Augusto Cespedes: El Pozo: the conflict between structure and
meaning.**
Peter Gold. *Romance Notes*, vol. 23, no. 2 (winter 1982),
p. 129-33.
Cespedes wrote about the Chaco War using the short story genre to understand
its impact on Bolivian society. Gold examines 'El Pozo,' the most frequently
recounted tale of the war. The tension between the story's structure and language
is so great that it tends to pull in opposite directions and this unlikely combination
makes the story successful.

696 **El minero en el moderno relato boliviano.** (The miner in the
modern Bolivian story.)
José Ortega. *Cuadernos Hispanoamericanos*, vol. 417 (March
1985), p. 26-32. bibliog.
This essay offers an overview of how the miner has been depicted in the modern
Bolivian novel.

# Novel

697 **The boom in Spanish American literature: a personal history.**
José Donoso, translated by Gregory Kolovakos. New York:
Columbia University Press, in association with the Center for
Inter-American Relations, 1977. 122p. bibliog.
Donoso, a participant in the contemporary Latin American literary boom,
explains why the novel became so popular in the 1960s and 1970s. This translation
of a work published in 1972, is full of personal insights. Although it is not directly
relevant to Bolivia, it is essential reading for anyone interested in this exciting
chapter of the region's literary development.

698 **Children of the Incas.**
David Mangurian. New York: Four Winds Press, 1979. 73p.
A thirteen-year-old boy, a Quechua Indian, who lives near Lake Titicaca,
describes his family, home and daily activities.

699 **The emergence of the Latin American novel.**
Gordon Brotherston. Cambridge, New York: Cambridge
University Press, 1977. 164p. bibliog.

A good general introduction to the Spanish-American novel. There are eight chapters and each deals with a different author. There is also a chapter devoted to José Maria Arguedas.

700 **Escritores bolivianos contemporaneos.** (Contemporary Bolivian
writers.)
Ricardo Pastor Poppe. La Paz: Editorial los Amigos del Libro,
1980. 192p. bibliog.

A brief introduction to contemporary Bolivian writers and literature. Provides biographical sketches of 37 writers, (3-5 pages each), which list their major works. Authors included are: Yolanda Bedregal, Adolfo Cáceres, Peter Levy, Juan Recacoechea, Pedro Shimose and Fernando Vaca Toledo.

701 **La novela social de Bolivia.** (The social novel in Bolivia.)
Evelio Echevarría. La Paz: Difusión, 1973. 2nd ed. 257p.
bibliog.

A good introduction to the Bolivian social protest novel. Each chapter examines a different type of novel. Included here are: the *indigenista* novel, the mine novel, the Chaco War novel, the novel of the tropics and the mestizo and political novels. Contains a good bibliography.

702 **La nueva narrativa boliviana: aproximación a sus aspectas
formales.** (The new Bolivian narrative: an approach to its formal
aspects.)
Oscar Rivera Rodas. La Paz: Camarlinghi, 1972. 218p.

A good introduction to an important Bolivian literary movement of the late 1960s. The writings of Renato Prada, Gaston Suarez, Jesus Urzagasti, Raul Teixido, Julio de la Vega and Arturo von Vacano are discussed here.

703 **Paisaje y novela en Bolivia.** (Region and novel in Bolivia.)
Reinaldo Alcázar V. La Paz: Difusión, 1973. 177p. bibliog.

Studies the role played by regions of Bolivia in the national novel. Each chapter addresses itself to a different locale: the Altiplano, the valleys, the Yungas, the jungle and the Chaco areas.

704 **Panorama y bibliografía de la novela social boliviana.** (Overview
and bibliography of the Bolivian social novel.)
Evelio Echevarría. *Interamerican Review of Bibliography*,
vol. 27, no. 2 (1977), p. 143-52. bibliog.

Novels of social protest in Bolivia follow certain clear themes: the Indians, miners and mines, the Chaco War, the jungle, the *cholo* or person of mixed blood and politics.

149

705 **Temas sobra la moderna narrativa boliviana.** (Themes in the
modern Bolivian narrative.)
José Ortega.   Cochabamba: Editorial los Amigos del Libro, 1973.
99p.

A collection of critical essays, by a noted specialist of the Bolivian narrative,
which examines the major themes presented in the 20th-century Bolivian novel.
Subjects discussed include: the Chaco War theme, and the individual careers of
Augusto Cespedes, Jesus Lara, Renata Prada, Fernando Vaca Toledo, and
others.

# Drama

706 **Teatro boliviano.** (Bolivian theatre.)
Raul Salmon.   Madrid: Paraninfo, 1972, 213p.

Three Bolivian plays are presented here: 'Viva Belzu', 'Tres Generalies' and
'Juana Sanchez'. A brief history of the Bolivian modern theatre precedes the
plays.

707 **Teatro boliviano contemporáneo.** (Contemporary Bolivian theatre.)
Willy Oscar Munoz.   PhD dissertation, University of Iowa, Iowa
City, 1979. 228p. bibliog.

Discusses the Bolivian national theatre during the period 1920 to 1970.

708 **Teatro inca: la escena enraizada.** (Inca theatre: the established
scene.)
Hernán González Bosque.   *Cuadernos Hispanoamericanos*,
vol. 328 (Oct. 1977), p. 116-30. bibliog.

Re-examines the pre-Columbian theatre and includes discussions on rituals,
dance, languages and the use of masks.

709 **Teatro virreinal en Bolivia.** (Viceregal theatre in Bolivia.)
Teresa Gisbert.   La Paz: Dirección Nacional de Informaciones,
1965. 35p.

Examines the 17th-century theatre. The author includes brief discussions on
comedies, theatre in Indian languages, the tragedies, the works of Diego Occina,
miner writers of Charcas, and Spanish dramatists in Charcas.

# Poetry

710 **Indice de la poesía boliviana contemporánea.** (Index of con-
temporary Bolivian poetry.)
Juan Quiroz. La Paz: Librería y Editorial 'Juventud', 1965. 438p.
An index of forty-one Bolivian poets who have made a substantial contribution to
Bolivian literature. The listing includes examples of their writings.

711 **Poesía de Bolivia, de la época precolombina al modernismo.** (Poetry
of Bolivia, from the pre-Columbian epoch to modernism.)
Yolanda Bedregal de Conitzer. Buenos Aires: Editorial
'Universitaria de Buenos Aires', 1964. 119p.
Using historical periodization, the author presents the writings of leading Bolivian
poets within the context of Bolivian national evolution.

712 **South America of the poets.**
Selden Rodman, illustrated by Bill Negron. New York:
Hawthorn Books, 1970. 270p. map.
Presents a uniquely informal and interesting portrait of the South America the
tourist, salesman or diplomat rarely sees. Indeed, it is from South American
artists and poets that we can learn the most. Poetry, for example, is deeply woven
into the fabric of these 'technologically backward' societies; it is even unusual to
find political figures who are not poets. The book attempts to instruct the tourist
and reader in the nature of South American culture and values by surveying poets
and poetry. Chapter four deals with Altiplano society.

# Short stories

713 **Antología del cuento boliviana.** (Anthology of the Bolivian short
story.)
Edited by Armando Soriano Badani. La Paz: Editorial los
Amigos del Libro, 1975. 438p.
This anthology is useful to the literary historian. The coverage of the 1900-50
period is more extensive than the post-1950 period.

714 **Bolivia en el cuento. Antología de ayer y de hoy.** (Bolivia and the
short story. Anthology of yesterday and today.)  .
Edited by Néstor Taboada Terán.   Buenos Aires: Editorial
'Convergencia', 1976. 119p.
This useful summary of the Bolivian short story is arranged by themes: mines,
Indians, war and politics.

715 **Cuentos.** (Stories.)
Ricardo Jaimes Freyre.   La Paz: Instituto Boliviano de Cultura,
1975. 55p.
A collection of modernist short stories originally published between 1896 and
1907.

716 **Cuentos bolivianos contemporáneos. Antología.** (Contemporary
Bolivian stories. Anthology.)
Edited by Hugo Lyeron Alberdi, Ricardo Pastor Poppe.   La Paz:
Ediciones Carmarlinghi, 1976. 201p.
Includes eleven contemporary short stories, each written by a different author.

# Legends and folk tales

717 **Black rainbow: legends of the Incas and myths of ancient Peru.**
John Bierhorst.   New York: Farrar, Straus & Gix, 1976. 131p.
bibliog.
A collection of ancient tales and legends of the Inca empire.

718 **Con la muerte a cuestas y otros cuentos**. (Death sleep and other
stories.)
Raúl Botelho Gosálvez.   La Paz: Difusión, 1975. 195p.
(Colección Vereda).
The theme of the encroachment of modernity and development on indigenous
Bolivian literature is repeated here in varied settings: the city, the mountains, the
jungles and the Yungas:

719 **Fantásticas aventuras del Atoj y el Diguillo.** (Fables in the Quechua
language.)
Manuel Robles Alarcón.   Lima: the author, 1975. 149p.
A collection of ten native folk tales which were collected by the author in the
1940s, and adapted for children's theatre in 1943 (they were first published in
1966). Ideal for children, these tales reflect native values and represent part of a
national attempt to rediscover the past.

720 **Florecillas y espinillas: rarisima colección boliviana de pensamientos humorísticos.** (Flowers and thorns: a rare collection of Bolivian humour.)
Alfonso Prudencio Claure.    La Paz: Dismo, 1973. 186p.
An anthology of humour.

721 **From oral to written expression: the native Andean chronicles of the early colonial period.**
Rolena Adorno.    Syracuse, New York: Maxwell School of Citizenship and Public Administration, 1982. 181p. bibliog.
Presents native legends, chronicles and folk tales in Spanish and English texts.

722 **Las mejores tradiciones y leyendas de Bolivia.** (The best folk tales and legends of Bolivia.)
Antonio Paredes Candia.    La Paz: Editorial 'Popular', 1979. 399p.
A collection of well-illustrated folk tales and legends. The author is a recognized expert who has published numerous articles and books on the folk culture of Bolivia.

723 **The singing mountaineers: songs and tales of the Quechua people.**
José María Arguedas, edited and with an introduction by Ruth Stephan, illustrated by Donald Weismann.    Austin, Texas: University of Texas, 1957. 203p. bibliog.
This study is confined to the literary aspects of folklore. The tales included are: 'The head of the town and the demon'; 'The condor's lovers'; 'Miguel Wayapa'; 'The snake's sweetheart'; and 'Isicha Puytu'. The author also gives an overview of Andean festivals, together with an examination of the role of songs and tales in native culture. For an analysis of the music included in this study see *La musique des Inca et ses survivances* by Rauol Harcourt. A list of recordings available is also included.

724 **La tradición oral en Bolivia.** (Oral tradition in Bolivia.)
Edited by Delina Anibarro de Halushka.    La Paz: Instituto Boliviano de Cultura, 1976. 458p.
A collection of over one hundred folk tales from Sucre, Potosí and Cochabamba, grouped by region, language, themes and symbolic content. These tales, in Aymará and Quechua, are stories introduced into the region by the Spanish during the colonial period. This is the best book available on Bolivian folk literature.

# Art

## Pre-Columbian

### General

725 **Pre-Columbian art history: selected readings.**
Jean Stearn, Alana Cordy-Collins.   Palo Alto, California: Peck
Publications, 1977. 519p.

A general introduction to pre-Columbian art history, which includes eighteen
essays on Mesoamerican art and fifteen essays on Andean art.

726 **Vanishing art of the Americas.**
Pál Kelemen.   New York: Walker, 1977. 232p.

A high quality production with excellent photographs. This volume relates nine
examples of art located in outlying regions which are vanishing through general
neglect and lack of interest.

### Textiles

727 **The cloth of the Quechuas.**
Grace Goodell.   In: *Man's many ways*. New York: Harper &
Row, 1973, p. 160-72.

An excellent, popular introduction to the art of highland weaving in Bolivia and
Peru. Designs, techniques and dyes are discussed here.

728 **Weaving traditions of highland Bolivia: [exhibition] December 19, 1978 to February 4, 1979.**
Guest curators, Laurie Adelson, Bruch Takami. Los Angeles: Craft and Folk Art Museum, 1978. 65p.
A superbly illustrated catalogue with much information on regional weaving techniques, patterns and motifs.

# Colonial

## General

729 **Arte virreinal en Potosí: fuentes para su historia.** (Viceregal art in Potosí, sources for its history.)
Mario Chacón Torres. Seville: Escuela de Estudios Hispano-americanos de Sevilla, 1973. 329p. (Publicaciones de Escuela de Estudios Hispano-americanos de Sevilla, 213).
This is the first systematic treatment of the art of colonial Potosí and deals with painting, architecture, sculpture, and silver making.

## Architecture

730 **Arquitectura andina, historia y analysis.** (Andean architecture, history and analysis.)
José de Mesa, Teresa Gisbert. La Paz: Colleción Arsanz y Vela, Embajada de España en Bolivia, 1985. 376p. maps. bibliog.
The best survey of colonial architecture available, and a work Mesa and Gisbert have been researching for over twenty years. Subjects covered include: the architecture of humanism; the Jesuits; and baroque style, mestizo style and late colonial style architecture. This work also surveys all major styles and movements from the 1530s to 1800. An excellent work which is of use to both art historians and social historians.

731 **Arquitectura virreinal en Bolivia.** (Viceregal architecture in Bolivia.)
Harold E. Wethe. La Paz: Instituto de Investigaciones Artísticas, 1961. 145p.
An overview of civil and religious architecture from the 16th to the 19th centuries. Chapters include: 'Sucre in the 18th century'; 'The mestizo style of La Paz, Potosí and Chuquisaca'; and '*Retablos* and civil architecture'.

155

732 **Bolivia: monumentos historicos arquelógicos.** (Bolivia: historical and archaeological monuments.)
José de Mesa, Teresa Gisbert. Mexico: Instituto Panamericano de Geografía e Historia, 1970. 146p.

A comprehensive survey of Bolivian colonial architecture. Includes an excellent bibliography, 110 photographs, details of Bolivian legislation on artistic patrimony, and a list of national monuments.

733 **Contribuciones al estudio de la arquitectura andina.** (Contributions to the study of Andean architecture.)
José de Mesa, Teresa Gisbert. La Paz: Academia Nacional de Ciencias de Bolivia, 1966. 102p.

A collection of five essays dealing with various aspects of colonial architecture in Bolivia: the chapel at Copacabana; the Church of St. Teresa, Cochabamba; the mestizo style of architecture; the meaning of the term 'mestizo style'; and the mestizo style in the Collao region.

734 **Iglesias de Oruro.** (Churches of Oruro.)
José de Mesa, Teresa Gisbert. La Paz: Dirección Nacional de Informaciones, 1962. 53p.

An illustrated survey of colonial church architecture in Oruro, Bolivia.

735 **The imperiled treasures of Potosí.**
Leonor Blum. *Americas* (OAS), vol. 32, no. 2 (1980), p. 13-17.

Sketches the history of Potosí and calls for the restoration of its baroque architecture.

# Sculpture

736 **Escultura virreinal en Bolivia.** (Viceregal sculpture in Bolivia.)
José de Mesa, Teresa Gisbert. La Paz: Academia Nacional de Ciencias de Bolivia, 1972. 489p.

The best available source on this subject. Part one deals with sculpture in three chapters entitled: 'Sculpture of the low Renaissance', 'Mannerism' and 'Indian sculptors', which includes such masters as Gaspar de la Cueva. Part two deals with sculpture in wood, *retablos*, pulpits and funeral art.

# Painting

737 **Bernardo Bitti.**
José de Mesa, Teresa Gisbert.   La Paz: Dirección Nacional de
Informaciones, 1961. 30p.
An illustrated volume of the life and works of Bernardo Bitti, one of the most
important painters of colonial Charcas.

738 **Bitti: un pinor manerista en Sud America.** (Bitti: a mannerist
painter in South America.)
José de Mesa, Teresa Gisbert.   La Paz: División de Extensión
Universitaria, Instituto de Estudios Bolivianos, 1974. 116p.
The definitive study of the life and works of an important Jesuit painter who
worked in Upper Peru in the late 1500s.

739 **Gaspar de la Cueva.**
José de Mesa, Teresa Gisbert.   La Paz: Dirección Nacional de
Informaciones, 1963. 71p.
An illustrated guide to the paintings of the colonial artist, Gaspar de la Cueva.
Cueva employed his talents as a painter and sculptor throughout the viceroyalty
of Peru, beautifying the cathedrals.

740 **Historia de la pintura cuzquena.** (History of the Cuzco School of
Painting.)
José de Mesa, Teresa Gisbert.   Lima: Fundación Augusto N.
Wiese; Banco Wiese LIDO, 1982. 2 vols.
The best available source on the Cuzco School of Painting which dominated
religious painting in the colonial period. Volume one discusses 17th-century
mannerism, the Cuzco School in the 19th century, the Jesuits, the transition to the
baroque style, the Flemish School, Indian painters, mural painting, techniques
and themes, and iconography. Volume two contains illustrations.

741 **Holguin y la pintura virreinal en Bolivia.** (Holguin and viceregal
painting in Bolivia).
José de Mesa, Teresa Gisbert.   La Paz: Librería y Editorial
'Juventud', 1977. 358p. bibliog.
The definitive work on painting in colonial Charcas. This is an updated version of
an earlier study and includes extensive research undertaken since 1956. The
authors take as their subject the leading painter in colonial upper Peru.

742 **Leonardo Flores.**
José de Mesa, Teresa Gisbert.   La Paz: Biblioteca de Arte y
Cultura Boliviana, 1963. [not paginated].
An illustrated guide to the paintings of Flores, a colonial artist.

157

743 **Museos de Bolivia: Nacional, Moneda, Charcas, Catedral de Sucre, Murillo. Pintura.** (Museums of Bolivia: National, Moneda, Charcas, Cathedral of Sucre, Murillo. Painting.)
José de Mesa, Teresa Gisbert. La Paz: Fondo Nacional de Cultura, 1969. 180p.

An illustrated guide to the paintings housed in five museums in Bolivia.

744 **Pinacoteca de San Francisco, catalogo.** (A catalogue of the paintings of San Francisco.)
Teresa Gisbert. La Paz: Universidad Boliviana Mayor de San Andres, 1973. 58p.

An illustrated guide to ninety-nine paintings of a Franciscan convent, dating from the 17th century through to the 20th century. Contains twenty-eight photographs.

# Contemporary

## General

745 **Arte contemporáneo: pintores, escultores, y grabadores bolivianos: desarrollo de las artes y la estética; de la caricatura, Academia Nacional.** (Contemporary art; painters, sculptors, and engravers of Bolivia; development of the arts, aesthetics, and caricature, National Academy.)
Rigoberto Villarroel Claure. La Paz: Dirección Nacional de Informaciones, 1952. 131p.

Discusses all forms of art in contemporary Bolivia with specific attention to realism, decorative art and cubism.

746 **Pintores del siglo XIX.** (Nineteenth-century painters.)
José de Mesa. La Paz: Dirección Nacional de Informaciones, 1963. 58p. bibliog.

An illustrated guide to 19th-century painters and paintings.

747 **Pintura contemporánea, 1952-1962** (Contemporary painting, 1952-62).
José de Mesa, Teresa Gisbert. La Paz: Dirección Nacional de Informaciones, 1962. [not paginated].

An illustrated guide to painting and painters of the 1952-62 period.

## Sculpture

748 **Emiliano Lujon.**
La Paz: Dirección Nacional de Informaciones, 1962. [not paginated].
An illustrated guide to the sculptures of Emiliano Lujon.

749 **Marina Nuñez.**
La Paz: Dirección Nacional de Informaciones, 1962. [not paginated].
An illustrated guide to the modernist sculpture of Marina Nuñez.

# Folk art

## General

750 **Andean art: an endangered tradition.**
Roy Craven. *Americas* (OAS), vol. 30, no. 1 (1978), p. 41-47.
Comments on the exhibition of traditional arts and crafts from Bolivia, Peru, Ecuador and Colombia presented at the University of Florida. Discusses the effects of modernization upon such popular art forms and predicts that those techniques will soon be lost if measures are not taken to preserve traditional methods.

## Weaving

751 **The art of Bolivian highland weaving.**
Marjorie Cason, Adele Caholander. New York: Watson-Guptill, 1976. 216p. bibliog.
For those interested in craft weaving, this comprehensive study gives details on how to weave, using techniques common in Bolivia. The techniques described were documented during months of field-work in highland villages.

752 **Aymará weavings: ceremonial textiles of colonial and 19th century Bolivia.**
Laurie Adelson, Arthur Tracht. Washington, DC: Smithsonian Institution, Travelling Exhibition Service, 1983. 159p.
Asks the reader to imagine a world in which textiles are the most valued and

respected products of culture. Aymará weaving is part of a tradition dating back
to 2500 BC. Beautiful photographs and illustrations of cloth, garments, mantles,
bags and belts are included.

753 **Bolivian highland weaving of the eighteenth, nineteenth and
twentieth centuries.**
Kitty Higgins, David Kenny.   Toronto, Canada: Canadian
Museum of Carpets and Textiles, 1978, 29p. bibliog.

A catalogue from an exhibition of folk weavings from Bolivia which were
collected by the authors. It contains many valuable photographs and discussions
of weaving techniques.

# Pottery

754 **South American folk pottery: traditional techniques from Peru,
Ecuador, Bolivia, Venezuela, Chile, Colombia.**
Gertrude Litto.   New York: Watson-Guptill, 1976. 224p. bibliog.

Surveys pottery techniques in existence today in the west coast republics of South
America.

# Music

755  **El arte folklórico de Bolivia.** (Bolivian folk art.)
Manuel Rigoberto Paredes.   La Paz: Gamarra, 1949. 151p.
A discussion of native music, choreography, instruments, music and dance of mestizo Bolivia.

756  **Cien danzas folkloricas y populares de Bolivia.** (One hundred folk and popular dances of Bolivia.)
Amalia Fernández de la Fuente, Susan Caballero de Cortes.
Sucre: Tupac Katari, 1972. 158p.
One hundred songs popular in the Chuquisaca area are arranged here for the piano.

757  **Compositores bolivianos.** (Bolivian composers.)
Peter Vásquez Messmer.   La Paz: Escuela de Artes y Gráficos Don Bosco, 1975. 76p.
Provides brief, impressionistic biographies of ten composers from La Paz, Oruro, Potosí, Cochabamba, Tarija, Sucre and Santa Cruz. The author focuses on the modern period (composers born after 1831) and, therefore, tends to omit some of the better composers.

758  **The evidence of the panpipe for prehistoric trans-Pacific contact.**
Roselle Tekiner.   Vienna: Archiv für Völkerkunde. Museum für Völkerkunde in Wien und von Verein Freunde der Völkerkunde, vol. 31, 1977, p. 7-132.
A definitive study of seventy panpipes in twenty US and European museums. The double row panpipe which is constructed so as to permit the blowing of two notes at the same time, the notes being an octave apart, occurs only in South America,

161

and in Melanesia. The double row panpipe flute is the traditional musical instrument of Bolivian folk music.

759 **Folklore Tarijeño.** (Tarija folklore.)
Wilson Mendieta Pacheco. La Paz: Gutenburg, 1962. 92p.
Presents music, legends, dances and customs from Tarija, Bolivia.

760 **Melodias y canciones de Tarija, 1574-1974.** (Melodies and songs of Tarija, 1574-1974.)
Leon Aurliano Auza. Tarija, Bolivia: Comité de Obras Publicas y Desarrollo de Tarija, 1974. 44p.
A leading Bolivian composer presents piano-vocal scores (which he has arranged) for forty historically popular songs.

761 **Music in Latin America, an introduction.**
Gérard Béhague. Englewood Cliffs, New Jersey: Prentice-Hall, 1979. 369p. bibliog. (Prentice Hall History of Music Series).
Deals with the 'art music' of Spanish-speaking Latin America. The author's emphasis is clearly on the 20th century (chapters 5-10) and less attention is paid to the 19th century (chapter 4). Its main contribution is to place the music of contemporary Latin America on a par with European music. Each chapter ends with extensive notes.

762 **Musical and other sound instruments of the South American Indians: a comparative ethnographical study.**
Karl Gustav Izikowitz. East Ardsley, England: S. R. Publishers, 1970. 433p.
This is a systematic classification of musical instruments, such as drums, clappers, trumpets and rattles, and the author's objective is to provide a better understanding of civilizations that did not produce written histories.

763 **New currents in *música folklórica* in La Paz, Bolivia.**
Gilka Wara Céspedes. *Latin American Music Review*, vol. 5, no. 2 (fall-winter 1984), p. 217-42.
An interesting, readable review of the current scene in folk music, its preservation, performance and innovations.

764 **Vivencias: poesía y composiciones musicales.** (Living experiences: poetry and musical compositions.)
Asunta Kimpias de Parada. La Paz: Editorial 'Casa Municipal de la Cultura', 1979. 308p.
An anthology of eighty-six poems, forty-one of which are preceded by folkloric melodies.

# Media

765 **Licensing newsman: the Bolivian experience.**
Jerry Knudson. *Gazette* (The Netherlands), vol. 25, no. 3 (1979),
p. 163-75.
In 1972 the régime of Hugo Banzer issued a decree which required the licensing
of all journalists. This procedure was supported by newsmen who wished to
professionalize their activities and also to improve their economic position in
Bolivia.

766 **Rural radio in Bolivia – a case study.**
R. J. Gwyn. *Journal of Communication*, University of North
Carolina, Chapel Hill, vol. 33, no. 2 (1983), p. 79-87.
Indigenous radio stations have assumed an important role in local communication
networks by adapting their information capabilities to community needs.

# Recreation

767 **Des loisirs pour une civilisation.** (Leisure activities for a
civilization.)
Michel Peltier. *Écrits de Paris*, vol. 345 (1975), p. 26-32.

Social customs of the descendants of the Incas continue in modern Bolivia and
Peru. The governments are attempting to preserve these traditional forms of
recreation.

# Science

768 **La ciencia en Bolivia; siglos xvii y xviii.** (Science in Bolivia; the
17th and 18th centuries.)
José de Mesa, Teresa Gisbert.   La Paz: Dirección Nacional de
Informaciones, 1962. 27p.
A brief introduction to scientific knowledge in the colonial era, written for the
non-scientist.

769 **Photoinhibition and the diurnal variation of phytoplankton photo-
synthesis in tropical, alpine Lake Titicaca (Peru-Bolivia).**
Patrick James Neale.   PhD dissertation, University of California,
Davis, 1984. 185p. bibliog.
Examines photosynthesis and plankton development in Lake Titicaca, a large,
deep, high altitude lake in the Andes of Peru and Bolivia.

# Culture

770 **La cultura nativa en Bolivia, su entronque y sus rasgos principales.**
(Native culture in Bolivia: its cognation and its principal
characteristics.)
Carlos Ponce Sanginés. La Paz: Instituto Boliviana de Cultura,
1975. 112p. bibliog.
A careful and readable introduction to the indigenous culture of modern Bolivia,
which traces its survival, growth and evolution from 1200 to 1970.

771 **A cultural history of Spanish America: from conquest to
Independence.**
Mariano Picon Salas. Berkeley, California: University of
California Press, 1962. 192p.
A classic work on the cultural evolution of Latin America. A select bibliography
is included (p. 176-79).

772 **La filosofía en Bolivia.** (Philosophy in Bolivia.)
Guillermo Franovich. La Paz: Librería y Editorial 'Juventud',
1966. 2nd. ed. 247p. bibliog.
Surveys Bolivia's rich intellectual tradition. Brief chapters sketch Bolivian thinking from the pre-Columbian period to the early 20th century. Over seventy-five
per cent of the book deals specifically with colonial and 19th-century thinkers and
ideas.

773 **Historia de la cultura boliviana: fundamentos socio-políticos.**
(History of Bolivian culture: socio-political fundamentals.)
José Fellmann Velarde.   La Paz: Editorial los Amigos del Libro,
1976. 497p.

A comprehensive list of persons and works important to the cultural history of Bolivia. Perhaps the best starting place for the scholar interested in the cultural evolution of Bolivia.

774 **Jaime Mendoza and the new Bolivia.**
Fernando Ortiz Sanz.   *Americas*, vol. 28, no. 9 (1976), p. 21-26.

Discusses the career of Jaime Mendoza, a leading Bolivian intellectual of the 1920s.

775 **Vicente Pazos Kanki, un boliviano en la libertad de América.**
(Vicente Pazos Kanki, a Bolivian in independent America.)
Charles Harwood Bowan, translated by Raul Mariaca G. Samuel
Mendoza. La Paz: Editorial los Amigos del Libro, 1975. 340p.
bibliog.

A biography of an important Bolivian thinker, Vicente Pazos Kanki (1779-1853), who was both a journalist and historian.

# Bibliographies

**776 Agrarian reform in Latin America: an annotated bibliography.**
Land Tenure Center staff. Madison, Wisconsin: Land Tenure
Center, University of Wisconsin Press, 1974. 667p.
The most comprehensive bibliography available on the highly important subject
of land reform in Latin America.

**777 The Andean Pact: a selected bibliography.**
Elizabeth G. Ferris. *Latin American Research Review*, vol. 13,
no. 3 (1978), p. 108-24.
The creation of the Andean Pact in 1968 brought waves of official commentary
and academic analyses. Scholars have approached the study of the Pact from
different academic disciplines, ideological positions and methodological backgrounds. The literature is essentially descriptive in nature.

**778 An annotated registry of scholarly journals in Hispanic studies.**
David William Foster. *Inter-American Review of Bibliography*,
vol. 28, no. 2 (1978), p. 131-47.
A list of seventy-six scholarly journals in the area of Hispanic studies. This is a
useful tool for the 'publishing scholar'.

**779 Archives and manuscripts on microfilm in the Nettie Lee Benson
Latin American collection: a checklist.**
Jane Garner. Austin, Texas: University of Texas Press, 1980.
48p.
A listing and guide to 6,300 reels of microfilm.

168

780  The Béeche, Gutiérrez and René-Moreno 'Bibliotecas Americanas':
     libraries and intellectual life in the nineteenth-century Andes.
     Gertrude M. Yeager.  *Inter-American Review of Bibliography*,
     vol. 31, no. 4 (1981), p. 507-13.
Examines the formation of libraries in Chile and Bolivia in the 19th century. The
careers of José Rosendo Gutiérrez of La Paz and Gabriel René-Moreno, a
Bolivian who lived in Santiago, Chile, are discussed.

781  **Bibliografía de la lengua guaraní.** (Bibliography of the Guaraní
     language.)
     José T. Medina.   Buenos Aires: Tallares Casa Jacabo Peuser,
     1930. 93p.
A basic bibliography of the Guaraní language. It is arranged in chronological
order and lists works which appeared between the 1530s and the 1920s. The
introductory essay describes the origins of the name 'Guaraní' and gives a history
of the study of the Guaraní language.

782  **Bibliografía de las lenguas quechua y aymará.** (Bibliography of the
     Quechua and Aymará languages.)
     José T. Medina.   New York: Museum of the American Indian,
     1930. 117p.
A standard reference source on native languages of the Andean region by a noted
Chilean historian and bibliographer.

783  **Bibliografía selectiva de las culturas indígenas de América.**
     (A selective bibliography of the indigenous cultures of America.)
     Juan Comas.   Mexico City: Instituto Panamericano de Geografía
     e Historia, Comisión de Historia, 1953. 292p.
This volume is organized into cultural areas (Mesoamerica, tropical, Andean) and
covers the fields of ethnography, linguistics, history, prehistory, archaeology, and
physical anthropology.

784  **Bibliographie des langues aymará et kičua.** (A bibliography of the
     Aymará and Quechua languages.)
     Paul Rivet.   Paris: Institut d'Ethnologie, Université de Paris,
     1951-65. 4 vols.
This bibliography is arranged chronologically by century and covers the period
1540-1875. The entries give detailed bibliographical and physical descriptions of
the relevant works and the work also includes a list of maps with their library
locations. The introduction is in French.

785 **Bibliography of the Andean countries: a selected current annotated bibliography relating to Peru, Bolivia, and Ecuador, drawn from reasonably accessible works published in English and Spanish.**
New York: American Universities Field Staff, 1958. 220p. (South American Series).
A dated but still useful bibliography of the Andean region.

786 **Bibliography of philosophy in the Iberian colonies of America.**
Walter B. Redmond. The Hague: Martinus Nijhoff, 1972. 175p. bibliog. (International Archives of the History of Ideas, no. 51).
A highly useful catalogue of over 800 listings of philosophy manuscripts and essays from the colonial era.

787 **Bolivia.**
Rosa Quintero Mesa. Ann Arbor, Michigan: University Microfilms, 1972. 156p. (Latin American Serial Documents Series, vol. 6).
An inclusive bibliography of Bolivian serials documents published since Independence, which are held in US and Canadian libraries. The entries are arranged alphabetically.

788 **Catálogo de la bibliografía boliviana; libros y folletos, 1900-1963.**
(Catalogue of Bolivian bibliographies, books and pamphlets, 1900-63.)
Arturo Costa de la Torre. La Paz: Universidad Boliviana Mayor de San Andrés, 1966. 2 vols.
An excellent listing of works written in Bolivia.

789 **The Catholic left in Latin America: a comprehensive bibliography.**
Therrin C. Dahlin, Gary Gillum, Mark Grover. Boston, Massachusetts: G. K. Hall, 1981. 410p.
An excellent research tool for those interested in the political activities of the Catholic Church in Latin America. The Bolivian section (p. 163-69) contains seventy-two citations of essentially periodical literature in the Catholic press, such as *(The) Americas, Catholic Messenger* and *Commonwealth*, among others.

790 **A critical survey of the literature on the Aymará language.**
Lucy Briggs. *Latin American Research Review*, vol. 14, no. 3 (1979), p. 87-105.
Describes major bibliographical sources, together with pre-linguistic and linguistic studies of the Aymará languages from colonial times to the present.

791  **Diccionario de la literatura boliviana.** (Dictionary of Bolivian
literature.)
José Ortega.   La Paz: Editorial los Amigos del Libro, 1977.
337p.
A comprehensive reference guide to Bolivian literature, providing bio-
bibliographical information about some 280 Bolivian writers.

792  **Doctoral dissertations in Hispanic American literature, a bibliography of dissertations completed in the United States.**
Barbara J. Robinson.   Austin, Texas: University of Texas Press,
1979. 49p.
A basic reference source for literary studies.

793  **Ecclesiastical archives of the Parroquias de Nuestra Senora de La
Paz, Bolivia 1548-1940: description and analysis.**
Nelly S. González.   *(The) Americas* (Academy of American
Franciscan History), vol. 40, no. 1 (1983), p. 109-17.
Describes the contents of, and access to, parish archives in La Paz. This study is
valuable for those interested in both social and demographic history.

794  **Education in Latin America: a bibliography.**
Ludwig Lauerhaus, Vera Lucia Olivira.   Los Angeles: University
of California, Los Angeles, Latin American Center, 1980. 430p.
A comprehensive list of materials relating to education, with a section on Bolivia
(p. 190-98).

795  **Ensayo de una bibliografía general de los periódicos de Bolivia,
1825-1905.** (General bibliographical essay of Bolivian periodicals,
1825-1905.)
Gabriel Rene-Moreno.   Santiago de Chile: Universo, 1905. 344p.
Reviews all major newspapers, and provides information about the publishers,
editorial policy and publication dates. A thorough catalogue and an excellent
guide which was originally published as separate articles in various Chilean
reviews.

796  **Geneological historical guide to Latin America.**
Lyman DePlatt.   Detroit, Michigan: Gale Research, 1978. 273p.
An indispensable guide to those interested in genealogy and social history. Each
Latin American republic has its own chapter, in addition to several topical
chapters which include data on specific areas.

797 **A guide to selected diplomatic archives of South America.**
Ron Seckinger. *Latin American Research Review*, vol. 10, no. 1
(1975), p. 127-53.

A guide to notable diplomatic archives in Brazil, Argentina, Bolivia, Chile,
Colombia, Peru and Uruguay.

798 **Handbook of Latin American Studies.**
Edited by Dolores Mayano Martin. Gainesville, Florida:
University of Florida Press, 1952-78; Austin, Texas: University of
Texas Press, 1979-. annual.

The most extensive and important bibliographical tool in Latin American studies.
The volumes alternate between the humanities and the social sciences.

799 **Information on music: a handbook of reference sources in European
languages. Vol. 2. The Americas.**
Guy A. Marco, with the assistance of Sharon Paugh Ferris, Ann
Garfield. Littleton, Colorado: Libraries Unlimited, 1977. 296p.

A highly selective bibliographical tool which includes material selected partly on
the basis of excellence and accessibility. This is the best starting point for any
researcher dealing with cultural material relating to the Western hemisphere. For
Bolivia, (items 965-974), the subjects covered include: folk music and folk song,
historical studies, musical instruments, and selective and critical guides.

800 **Latin America: a guide to illustrations.**
A. Curtis Wilgus. Metuchen, New Jersey: Scarecrow Press, 1981.
250p.

This guide to illustrations of Latin America has two sections of interest to
Bolivian scholars. Section four deals with pre-Inca and Inca civilization and
art catalogues, architecture, music, pottery and textiles. There is also a section
on colonial coinage. For Bolivia there are pictures of town and village life, transport,
religion and culture.

801 **Latin American economic and social serials.**
Committee on Latin America. London: Archon Books, 1969.
189p.

A comprehensive guide to serials dealing with economic and social issues. The
headings are broad and include general publications and those on specific areas.
Fifteen entries relate to Bolivia.

802   **Los mercedarios en Bolivia: documentos para su historia,**
      **1535-1975.** (Mercedarians in Bolivia: documents for their history,
      1535-1975.)
      Eudoxio de Jesus Palacco, Jose Brunet.   La Paz: Universidad
      Boliviana Mayor de San Andrés, 1977. 385p. bibliog.

An anthology of archival sources of the Mercedarians. Sources included here
relate to Indians, blacks, *haciendas* and friars.

803   **Protestantism in Latin America: a bibliographical guide.**
      Edited by John H. Sinclair.   South Pasadena, California: William
      Carey Library, 1976. 414p.

A comprehensive annotated bibliography of selected references, mainly in
English, Spanish and Portuguese.

804   **Recent research on Andean peasant revolts, 1750-1820.**
      Leon Campbell.   *Latin American Research Review*, vol. 14, no. 1
      (1979), p. 3-43.

Describes the various indigenous revolts of the late colonial period in the Andean
region prior to the Túpac Amaru uprising in 1780, and provides a bibliography on
the subject.

805   **Research collections of Chile's Instituto Nacional**
      Gertrude M. Yeager.   *Americas* (forthcoming).

During the 19th century and until the 1920s, Chile's Instituto Nacional, a national
secondary school, housed one of the most extensive American libraries in South
America. This note discusses the contents of the contemporary library which has
an extensive section on Bolivia, the result of Rene-Moreno's long tenure as
librarian there.

806   **Revolution and structural change in Latin America: a bibliography**
      **on ideology, development and the radical left (1930-1965).**
      Ronald Chilcote.   Standford, California: Hoover Institution on
      War, Revolution and Peace, 1970. 2 vols.

The major headings include agrarian reform, anti-Communism, Christian
democracy and economic development. There are also sections on individual
countries.

# Reference Works and Encyclopaedias

807 **A decade of political change in Latin America, 1963-1973.**
Raymond Estep.   Maxwell Air Force Base, Alabama: Air
University Institute for Professional Development of Documentary
Research, 1974. 321p. (Air University Documentary Research
Study).
A country-by-country analysis of all constitutional and non-constitutional changes
in government. Also, reviews all significant elections down to the municipal level
and describes the influence of strikes, guerrilla war and revolts on the political
process.

808 **Enciclopedia del arte en América.** (Encyclopaedia of American
art.)
Buenos Aires: Editorial Bibliográfico Argentina, 1969. 5 vols.
Volumes one and two provide an introduction to the history of art – painting,
sculpture and architecture – for each American republic. For Bolivia, see volume
one (p. 93-156).

809 **Encyclopedia of Latin America.**
Edited by Helen Delpar.   New York: McGraw-Hill, 1974. 651p.
Presents information concerning all aspects of Latin American society: art,
literature, biography, history, economics and politics.

810 **Latin American government leaders.**
David William Foster.   Tempe, Arizona: Center for Latin
Studies, Arizona State University, 1975. 135p.
Gives brief biographical sketches of contemporary political figures.

811  **Latin American governmental and political organization: an outline.**
Russell H. Fitzgibbon.  Pasadena, California: Current World
Leaders, 1973. 14p.

Presents in tabular-form concise information about the constitutions, government
departments, elections and political parties for each Latin American state.

812  **Monografía de Bolivia.** (Monograph of Bolivia.)
Comité Nacional del Sesquicentenario de la República.  La Paz:
Dirección Nacional de Informaciones, 1975. 4 vols.

A comprehensive and well-written reference manual which covers geography,
archaeology, sociology, popular culture, economics and history.

813  **Nomenclature and hierarchy – basic Latin American legal sources.**
Rubens Medina, Cecilia Medina-Quiroga with the editorial assist-
ance of Sandra A. Sawicki.  Washington, DC: Library of
Congress, 1979. 123p. bibliog.

Identifies the hierarchy of the legal institutions of each Latin American nation,
thereby providing valuable legal information relevant to each country. (Available
from the Superintendant of Documents, US Government Printing Office).

# Dictionaries

814 **Diccionario del *cholo* ilustrado.** (Illustrated dictionary of
Bolivianisms.)
Alfonso Prudencio Claure.  La Paz: Ojo Publicaciones, 1978.
298p.
Examines the Bolivian-Spanish language with a special emphasis on provincial-
isms, wit and humour.

815 **The Latin American political dictionary.**
Ernest Rossi, Jack C. Plano.  Santa Barbara, California:
ABC-Clio Information Services, 1982. 273p.
Defines political terms and explains the significance of political events and
describes important concepts in Latin American area studies.

816 **Historical dictionary of Bolivia.**
Dwight B. Heath.  Metuchen, New Jersey: Scarecrow Press,
1962. 323p. bibliog. (Latin American Historical Dictionaries,
no. 4).
A convenient research manual for those beginning to study Bolivian national
development. It includes information about people and events of political
importance, as well as terms relevant to geographical, ethnographic, linguistic,
sociological and intellectual aspects of history. A substantial bibliographical essay
is appended.

# Index

The index is a single alphabetical sequence of authors (personal and corporate), titles of publications and subjects. Index entries refer both to the main items and to other works mentioned in the notes to each item. Title entries are in italics. Numeration refers to the items as numbered.

180

183

185

197

204

213

217

218

223

# Map of Bolivia

This map shows the more important towns and other features.

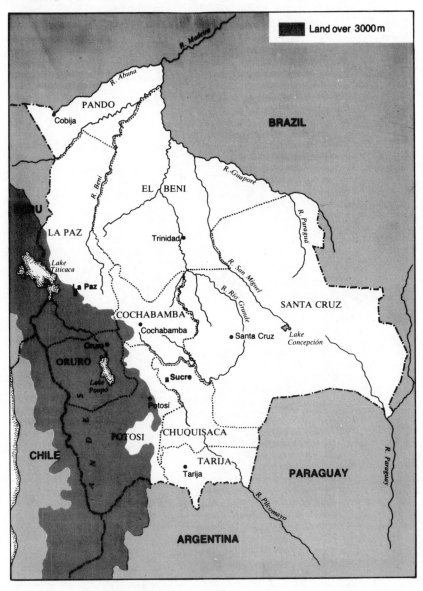

Land over 3000m

R. Madeira

R. Abuna

PANDO

Cobija

BRAZIL

R. Guaporé

R. Beni

EL BENI

PERU

LA PAZ

Trinidad

R. Paraguá

Lake Titicaca

La Paz

R. San Miguel

COCHABAMBA

Cochabamba

R. Río Grande

Santa Cruz

SANTA CRUZ

Lake Concepción

Oruro

ORURO

Lake Poopó

Sucre

Potosí

POTOSI

CHUQUISACA

CHILE

TARIJA

Tarija

PARAGUAY

R. Paraguay

R. Pilcomayo

ARGENTINA